The Protectors

The Story of the Food and Drug Administration

For over sixty years the Federal Food and Drug Administration has waged war against those who would endanger the consumer public. It has tracked down fraud, deception and adulteration of foods and medicines; countered the threats of pesticides and drugs such as LSD; attacked harmful cosmetics and the practices of certain drug companies; helped prosecute quack doctors peddling false hope with phony gadgets. Just what is the FDA? Why was it established? Who are its prime movers? How does it go about doing its special brand of detective work? All of these questions and more are covered in this dramatic and inspiring story of the unsung heroes who stand guard over our health and safety.

Books by Harry Edward Neal

Career

DISEASE DETECTIVES:
  Your Career in Medical Research
ENGINEERS UNLIMITED:
  Your Career in Engineering
MONEY MASTERS:
  Your Career in Banking
NATURE'S GUARDIANS:
  Your Career in Conservation
SKYBLAZERS:
  Your Career in Aviation
YOUR CAREER IN ELECTRONICS
YOUR CAREER IN FOREIGN SERVICE

Informational

COMMUNICATION:
  From Stone Age to Space Age
DIARY OF DEMOCRACY:
  The Story of Political Parties in America
FROM SPINNING WHEEL TO SPACECRAFT:
  The Story of the Industrial Revolution
MONEY
THE MYSTERY OF TIME
THE PROTECTORS:
  The Story of the Food and Drug Administration
SIX AGAINST CRIME:
  Treasury Agencies in Action
THE TELESCOPE
TREASURES BY THE MILLIONS:
  The Story of the Smithsonian Institution

The
PROTECTORS

The Story of the
Food and Drug Administration

by Harry Edward Neal

Illustrated with photographs

JULIAN MESSNER NEW YORK

Published simultaneously in the United States and Canada by
Julian Messner, a division of Simon & Schuster, Inc.,
1 West 39 Street, New York, N.Y. 10018. All rights reserved.

Printed in the United States of America
Library of Congress Catalog Card No. 68-25107

FOREWORD

WHEN I began to do research for this book and learned about serious cases involving poisoned foods, harmful drugs and cosmetics, I looked with some degree of suspicion upon my daily bread, milk, coffee and snacks, and even hesitated about taking pills my doctor had prescribed for a troublesome cold.

The deeper I dug into the subject, the less suspicious I became, and any misgivings I had were replaced by confidence in the knowledge that the Federal Food and Drug Administration (FDA) was making sure that food and drug products intended for my use were safe.

While I worked on my book, the FDA was somewhat in a state of flux. Reorganization was going on throughout the Department of Health, Education and Welfare.

Also, President Lyndon B. Johnson had recommended that the FDA's Bureau of Drug Abuse Control (BDAC) be transferred to the Department of Justice and combined with the Treasury's Bureau of Narcotics. By the time you read this, the transfers will probably have been made, but I have included material about the BDAC because it was an important function of the FDA and also because the facts about LSD, pep pills, tranquilizers and other drugs of abuse will apply regardless of what agency enforces the laws concerning them.

5

I invite your special attention to the leniency of our courts in sentencing offenders convicted of health frauds, of selling contaminated foods or marketing products containing hazardous substances without adequate warnings or "pushing" LSD and other harmful drugs. To an offender whose profits may total $50,000 or $100,000, is a fine of a thousand dollars any deterrent? Comparatively few have been compelled to serve prison sentences, even though their offenses may have resulted in serious injury or death to victims of their products.

The FDA and the public are deserving of greater support from our courts. When more severe sentences are imposed, the word will spread among other potential offenders, and when that happens, we may reasonably expect a decrease in the marketing of harmful drugs and cosmetics, poisonous food and hazardous substances.

The FDA has been and will undoubtedly continue to be criticized by many persons and firms affected by its regulations and decisions. No government regulatory body can please everybody. But in defense of the FDA, it should be said that this important agency is trying to do an effective job in behalf of the American consumer. It has admitted making some mistakes—but perfection in all things is rare where human fallibility is involved.

I concluded my research with a deep respect for the FDA and its people. You, of course, may have contrary feelings. I hope only that you'll read my book and enjoy it as a kind of commentary on our wonderful, progressive, frightening, poisonous world.

Harry Edward Neal

Culpeper, Virginia

CONTENTS

	Foreword	5
1.	Have a Pinch of Poison?	9
2.	The Tainted Trail	24
3.	Laws and Labels	43
4.	The Health Quacks	66
5.	Drug Dangers	80
6.	Bennies, Barbs, and Beedack	97
7.	LSD: Ticket to Tragedy	115
8.	Label Lures and Phony Cures	128
9.	Gadgets and Gimmicks	140
10.	Home and Health Hazards	148
11.	Helpers and Yelpers	162
	Sources of Further Information	183
	Index	

Have a Pinch of Poison?

AMONG the wonders of our fast-moving modern civilization, include this one: "I wonder why more people don't die from eating poisoned food, drinking contaminated liquids, using cosmetics containing dangerous chemicals, taking harmful drugs and falling prey to phony health quacks?"

Some do—die, that is. In Wisconsin, the owner of a hardware store bought a quantity of permanent-type antifreeze which, if swallowed, could kill a human being. To sell the antifreeze in small quantities the retailer poured it into secondhand jugs and bottles, including empty wine bottles that still bore the original labels. One of the wine bottles came into the hands of an old man who read the label and believed the contents to be wine. He drank some. A few hours later he died in agony.

In California, several small children came across small balls of various colors. Slightly larger than pea size, the balls resembled a popular colored breakfast food and also appeared to the youngsters to be a kind of candy. Actually they were crackerballs, a type of imported firecracker made only in Japan and Formosa. A number of the children tried to eat them, and the balls exploded, causing loosened teeth, serious burns and cuts in gums, tongues and cheeks. Pieces of crackerball shell were driven into tender mouth tissues.

A five-year-old girl in New York City found a lump of sugar in the refrigerator and ate it. Soon she began to scream and cry. At the hospital her stomach was pumped. Doctors discovered that the sugar cube had been treated with lysergic acid diethylamide, commonly known as LSD. It had been bought by her eighteen-year-old uncle in Greenwich Village, and he had put it in the refrigerator intending to eat it later. The doctors couldn't tell whether or not the little girl would suffer any permanent brain damage.

Bottles of a certain baby formula were seized in Colorado because it was discovered that the formula was contaminated with fragments of manure.

A Virginia company tried and failed to ship a quantity of a product labeled as "frozen deviled crabs." In part, pieces of flounder had been substituted for crabmeat; in addition, the weight of the package was less than the labels indicated.

Vibrators, vacuum cleaners, electronic "marvels" and a host of other weird devices were seized from health quacks who claimed the gadgets could cure or diagnose practically any disease, including cancer, tuberculosis, heart trouble and other serious ailments.

These are just a few of thousands of cases that have come to the attention of the Food and Drug Administration (FDA), an agency of the U. S. Department of Health, Education and Welfare (HEW).

The day-to-day work of the FDA saves millions of Americans from serious illness or death. Yet unfortunately its activities and aims are little known to the general public, because they hit the headlines only when some sensational episode unfolds—such as the discovery that the sedative thalidomide, when taken by pregnant women, could cause horrible deformities in newborn babies. The thalidomide story is told elsewhere in this book.

To understand the gigantic task and the obstacles facing the FDA now and in years gone by, one must dig into its beginnings and development—in itself a story of raw courage, frustration, persistence and dedication.

Since the beginning of civilized society, men have been concerned about the purity of their food and drink. In Europe, kings sometimes employed "tasters" who sampled food and drink before it was served to the rulers, to be sure that no assassin had poisoned the feast and that the servings had not been accidentally tainted.

In 1202 King John of England proclaimed the first English food law, the Assize of Bread. This made it illegal for bakers or others to adulterate bread by mixing into the flour such ingredients as ground peas or beans. Violators were put into the pillory "with a certain quantity of such dough hung from their necks."

An ancient Chinese writing shows that some two hundred years before Christ, "the Supervisors of Markets had agents whose duty it was to prohibit the making of spurious products, including food, and the defrauding of purchasers."

In India, a Sanskrit text written about 300 B.C. says, "Adulteration of grains, oils, alkalis, salts, scents and medicinal articles with similar articles of no quality shall be punished with a fine of twelve panas." The pana was a copper coin of small value.

Pierre Pomet, author of *The History of Druggs,* a French book published in 1650, wrote about drug adulteration: "It may be still more surprising to learn that this terrible evil is the most ordinary thing in the world, and that nothing is more common in the drug shops and apothecary shops than these falsified drugs."

In 1824, when it was discovered that some American bakers were careless about making bread containing adulterants, a Flour Inspection Act was passed in the District of Columbia.

A number of states enacted various kinds of food and drug laws, but these were binding only within each state's borders and were not at all uniform. Products that were unlawful in Pennsylvania might be quite legal in the adjoining state of New Jersey. Better controls were needed. The population of the United States was growing rapidly, new towns and cities were springing up, new mechanical inventions resulted in new products and new factories for their manufacture. Farmers left their land to work for wages in the cities. The industrial revolution was in full swing, and the nation's economy was changing from agricultural to industrial.

12

This economic change made it necessary to bring foods from distant areas to meet the demands of the increasing city populations. A boom in commercial food processing led to an extensive use of chemical food preservatives such as borax, formaldehyde (which undertakers also used for embalming corpses), and salicylates. Also, artificial colors and flavors, many of them harmful to humans, were used indiscriminately to make the "embalmed" foods more attractive in both taste and appearance. Labels on such foods made no mention of their ingredients.

Foods were not the only products consumed by a poisoned public. The market was flooded with thousands of so-called patent medicines, some dangerous, some harmless. Self-styled "doctors" traveled from town to town with wagonloads of "snake oil" and "elixirs of life," which often consisted of bitters spiked with whiskey, rum or gin—though never labeled as such. They staged "medicine shows," using a singer, magician, or some other entertainer to attract the townspeople, and when a crowd had gathered, the "doctors" went into eloquent spiels about their cure-alls, which they sold for fifty cents or a dollar a bottle. Some men and women who preached temperance and fought the sale and use of hard liquor were eager buyers of the alcoholic "elixirs," which they could drink without shame "for medicinal purposes."

Not all of the "cures" were alcoholic. Some that claimed to quiet crying babies contained opium or other deadly habit-forming drugs. Cocaine was often the major ingredient in "cures" for asthma and lung diseases. Some worthless preparations consisted entirely of a colored solution of sugar and water, and others that were guaranteed to "relieve" headaches endangered the health of sufferers through the use of dangerous coal-tar drugs. Thousands of children and adults died or became seriously ill as a result of taking the various "elixirs of life," which could be bought at almost every crossroads store.

Although many firms did make wholesome and reliable products, such so-called medicines as "Kickapoo Indian Sagwa" and "Warner's Safe Cure for Diabetes" reflected not only the limited medical knowledge of the times, but also the widely accepted doctrine of *caveat emptor*, a Latin phrase meaning, "Let the buyer beware." In other words, the person who buys any product does so at his own risk.

That there were plenty of buyers of worthless and dangerous "cures" was evident from the fact that many of those who made and peddled the stuff retired as multimillionaires. The buyers had no protection, since labels did not identify any ingredients, and warnings against overdoses were unheard of. The public learned only from bitter and often tragic experience.

The dangers in poisoned food and drugs were known to the state chemists, who were also aware of the lack or weakness of proper controls. Many of these chemists urged Congress to enact food and drug laws to protect the public's health, and from 1879 to 1906 more than one hundred such bills were introduced in Congress, with discouraging results. It was the leadership of one remarkable man, Dr. Harvey Washington Wiley, that finally made food and drug protection an effective function of the Federal government.

Dr. Wiley graduated from Hanover (Indiana) College in 1867, when he was twenty-two years old. After graduate study at Indiana Medical College, he earned a living by teaching Latin, Greek and chemistry in other schools, and in 1873 won a degree at Harvard University. During the next year, 1874, Purdue University was founded, and Wiley was appointed as its first professor of chemistry. He served there and as the state chemist of Indiana until 1883, when he accepted a post as chief chemist for the U. S. Department of Agriculture in Washington, D. C. It was there that Dr. Wiley began his uphill fight against adulterated foods and fraudulent drugs.

For a long time it was a one-sided fight, with heavy odds against Harvey Wiley. When the unscrupulous food and drug producers realized that they had a fighting opponent in an important official position in the Federal government, they did everything they could to discourage him and to weaken his resistance. Undaunted, Dr. Wiley continued his crusade. Tall and husky, broad of shoulder and chest, with piercing dark eyes, he made an impressive appearance and had a most persuasive manner. He was an excellent speaker, both lucid and forceful, and was soon in demand to lecture to civic organizations, women's clubs and other groups. His talks were designed to gain support in the interests of public health, and they became an effective weapon in his food and drug war.

In the course of Dr. Wiley's battle, some laws were passed that began to crack down on certain food and drug activities. In 1890, for example, new laws prohibited the *importing* of adulterated food and drugs, and provided for the certification of certain *exported* meat products. In July, 1902, Congress enacted a law prohibiting the false branding of food and dairy products. But the adulteration of domestic foods and the manufacture of harmful drugs continued.

In 1903 Dr. Wiley startled the whole country by announcing that he had organized a group of twelve volunteers from employees in his Bureau of Chemistry who would actually eat a variety of foods containing all sorts of preservatives and additives, to learn which foods, if any, were truly harmful to humans. The group quickly became known as the Poison Squad, and Dr. Wiley as Old Borax.

His experiments proved that many foods were adulterated and injurious, and various members of Congress became sufficiently impressed to call upon him for advice and suggestions about food-purity legislation. By this time a number of other people, including scientists, were concerned about poisons in food and drugs, and many of them also came to Wiley for help and counsel. A newspaper article in the New York *Sun* called him Chief Janitor and Policeman of the People's Insides.

Dr. Wiley had one answer for those who wanted to leave things as they were. "Just tell the truth on the labels," he said, "and let the consumers judge for themselves."

As Wiley's influence grew, so did the opposition. When Wiley kept pressing and clamoring for the enactment of Federal food and drug laws, Congressman James S. Sherman of New York was one of those who fought such action. Most government employees, even today, are reluctant to battle publicly with members of Congress, but Wiley wasn't. He charged that Sherman's opposition was selfish, because the congressman owned a cannery whose operations might be affected by restrictive laws, and he labeled Sherman Short Weight Jim.

Wiley's enemies in the food and drug industry spread their propaganda in newspapers and magazines. Articles claimed falsely that these manufacturers used only harmless chemicals as food preservatives and that dyes used as coloring matter were as safe as pure water.

Some makers of patent medicines, who paid large sums for advertising space in certain newspapers and magazines, notified these publications that such advertising would be canceled if any material was printed that was unfavorable to the patent-medicine industry. Fearful of losing this profitable business, many publishers refused to print stories exposing the use of harmful ingredients in elixirs, ointments, pills, potions, and powders. Others, however, refused to succumb to this form of blackmail.

A few national magazines, sympathetic to Wiley's cause, joined forces with him. *The Ladies' Home Journal, Good Housekeeping,* and *Collier's Weekly,* among others, helped to arouse public opinion through hard-hitting editorials, articles and cartoons.

Some of the reputable food and drug processors also supported Wiley's cause, realizing that sensible restrictions would help them and drive disreputable competitors out of business.

Probably Dr. Wiley's most powerfully ally was President Theodore Roosevelt, himself a crusader of no mean ability. On December 5, 1905, in his annual message to the Congress, Mr. Roosevelt included this statement:

I recommend that a law be enacted to regulate interstate commerce in misbranded and adulterated foods, drinks, and drugs. Such law would protect legitimate manufacturers and commerce, and would tend to secure the health and welfare of the consuming public. Traffic in foodstuffs which have been debased or adulterated so as to injure health or to deceive purchasers should be forbidden.

Dr. Wiley's arguments received a boost as the result of a novel written by Upton Sinclair and published in 1906 under the title, *The Jungle*. Presented as fiction, the book included descriptions of food-processing operations in Chicago packing houses. Here's one sentence: "The rats were nuisances; the packers would put poisoned bread out for them; they would die, and then rats, bread, and meat would go into the hoppers together."

The resulting publicity brought added public support for real action. In addition to news stories, the New York *Evening Post* carried this parody:

> Mary had a little lamb,
> And when she saw it stricken,
> She shipped it off to Packing Town
> And now it's labeled "Chicken."

Sinclair's publishers, Doubleday, Page & Company, for legal reasons, sent an attorney to take a firsthand look at the packing houses in Chicago to see whether or not the author's manuscript should be toned down before it was published. The lawyer reported that there was no exaggeration in *The Jungle,* and he wrote an article based upon his own observations.

This article, along with two others, eventually appeared in *The World's Work,* a magazine also published by (Doubleday, Page.) First, however, the publishers sent proofs of the articles to Theodore Roosevelt. Shocked by the revelations, the President appointed a commission to make a thorough investigation of the packing houses.

After its investigation this commission submitted a report, part of which read:

> We saw meat shovelled from filthy wooden floors, piled on tables rarely washed, pushed from room to room in rotten box carts, in all of which processes it was in the way of gathering dirt, splinters, floor filth, and the expectoration of tuberculous and other diseased workers.

The President's commission was promptly subjected to some of the same kind of abuse that had been heaped upon Dr. Wiley. Owners of the packing houses descended upon "friendly" congressmen and senators, seeking to discredit members of the commission. They also released floods of false propaganda to the press, making claims and denials that were flagrantly contradicted by the evidence.

The packers lost. So did the other unscrupulous food and drug manufacturers. In June, 1906, Congress almost unanimously approved the Food and Drugs Act and a Meat Inspection Act, both of which were signed into law by President Theodore Roosevelt on June 30. Dr. Wiley had won his first major victory. Quite appropriately, he has been called Father of the Pure Food and Drug Act.

Administration of the law was begun January 1, 1907, by the Bureau of Chemistry which Dr. Wiley headed in the Department of Agriculture. As he intensified his crackdown on the cheats, his enemies grew more desperate. Some had friends among congressmen and senators, others had "friends of friends" with political influence. In 1911 Wiley's opponents finally launched a whispering campaign to remove him from his post, spreading rumors that corruption and irregularities existed in his Bureau of Chemistry.

Certain members of Congress believed the false propaganda. Others, who must have known Wiley was right, chose to pretend he was wrong, in order to help their friends or to return political favors. The smear campaign was successful enough to result in official hearings, but they proved to be a boon, because the accusers couldn't produce the slightest concrete evidence to support their charges, and Dr. Wiley was completely vindicated.

Although Dr. Wiley retired as chief chemist in 1912, the men and women recruited by him—and by his successors—developed an efficient organization.

These dedicated people continued the development of scientific methods of analysis, still the foundation of food and drug protection.

They worked out legal procedures and the techniques of inspection, and applied them in hundreds of hard-fought court actions.

They won scores of judicial decisions which both strengthened the law and revealed its weaknesses.

They built strong precedents through administrative decisions and regulations.

In fighting for the consumer, they eventually won the respect of industry and a high degree of voluntary compliance.

Many young people in the Bureau of Chemistry found such satisfaction that they made the job their life work. Four of them later climaxed their careers as heads of the Food and Drug Administration.

In the years that followed passage of the original Food and Drugs Act of 1906, Congress enacted amendments to prohibit false and fraudulent labeling of medicines, and to require that quantity information be shown on food packages and net-weight labeling on meats.

In 1927 a separate law-enforcement agency was established, first known as the Food, Drug, and Insecticide Administration, later (in 1931) as the Food and Drug Administration, the name it still has.

In 1938 Congress passed the Federal Food, Drug and Cosmetic Act. The provisions in this law would have given great satisfaction to Harvey Wiley, but he had died in 1930 and was buried in Arlington National Cemetery. These were among some of the provisions of this 1938 act:

Extended coverage of the food and drug laws to cosmetics and devices;

Required safety clearance on new drugs before distribution;

Prohibited the addition of poisonous or harmful substances to foods except where required or unavoidable (and then in safe amounts);

Provided for tolerances for unavoidable or required poisonous substances;

Authorized standards of identity, quality, and fill of containers for food;

Authorized factory inspections; and

Added the remedy of court injunction to previous remedies of seizure and prosecution.

On July 1, 1940, the Food and Drug Administration was transferred from the Department of Agriculture to the Federal Security Agency (FSA). The FSA became the U. S. Department of Health, Education and Welfare (HEW) on April 11, 1953. The Food and Drug Administration (FDA) is still an agency of that department.

As this book was being written (in 1968), the FDA was headed by Commissioner James L. Goddard, a physician, former assistant surgeon general of the U. S. Public Health Service and chief of the Communicable Disease Center in his home town of Atlanta, Georgia.

In February, 1966, shortly after his appointment to FDA, Dr. Goddard appeared before a Congressional subcommittee to testify in connection with his agency's proposed appropriation for the following fiscal year. Two members of this subcommittee were Congressmen Daniel J. Flood of Pennsylvania and the late John E. Fogarty of Rhode Island. In the course of the hearing, these exchanges took place:

MR. FLOOD (to Dr. Goddard). How are you [the FDA] accepted by the general public, by the man in the street? Are you respectable? Does he know about you? Are you an organization of integrity? How does the average citizen look upon you?

DR. GODDARD. My knowledge of this tells me that the average citizen looks to us for his protection, and if he can purchase a product, then the Food and Drug Administration must have determined it was safe. He places great reliance on the agency and its activities.

MR. FOGARTY. I don't think this is an answer to Mr. Flood's question. I know what the answer is. The average person doesn't know what the Food and Drug Administration does. . . . If you stop ten people on the street, nine would not even know this administration exists. The main reason is that you do not have citizens' groups talking about what you are doing. You cannot do it yourself unless you get in the headlines because you closed down some pharmaceutical manufacturers or something like . . . the thalidomide incident.

DR. GODDARD. This did a great deal in raising the con-

22

fidence of the public, which is why I responded as I did
. . . and also the controversy over birth control pills and
the pesticide problem with foods. I am sure you are right
—we can walk across the street in Providence or my home
town of Atlanta and find the same problem—people not
knowing what the Food and Drug Administration does.

The story of what it does and how it does it is fascinating
and dramatic. The work is often exciting, sometimes dangerous, almost always impressive. To paraphrase Dr. Wiley,
read the pages ahead and judge for yourself.

2_____

The Tainted Trail

IN 1885 a physician, Dr. D. E. Salmon, identified an organism that causes a bacterial infection of the intestines in persons who eat food contaminated by it. The organism is called *Salmonella* (after Dr. Salmon) and is also known as paratyphoid bacillus. It has probably been among us since man first trod the earth.

Salmonellosis, the infection caused by the organism, usually results from man's own contamination of his environment. Some of us may have been its victims unknowingly, blaming our illness on "upset stomach" or "intestinal flu." For many victims there would be no serious consequences, but an outbreak of salmonellosis in a hospital, a school, or a nursing home for the elderly could be extremely serious. Gastroenteritis can kill the very young as well as the old.

Man is almost always infected by this germ as the result of eating contaminated foods. Within eight to forty-eight hours the victim develops nausea, vomiting, stomach pains, and persistent diarrhea. In most cases, after days of quiet suffering the symptoms subside, and the victim tells friends that he had an attack of the "twenty-four-hour flu." But some of those who are afflicted may become carriers of the organism and pass it along to others. It's estimated that in 1966 about two million Americans were stricken with salmonellosis.

More than twelve hundred types of *Salmonella* organisms are known to exist, and the list is not complete. Not only food-producing animals such as steers and hogs may be implicated in the spread of *Salmonella;* a wide variety of birds, reptiles, dogs, cats, flies, roaches, ticks, and other insects are active in the chain of infection.

During one period the FDA discovered that some 26 percent of all shipments of liquid, frozen, or dried eggs examined were contaminated with *Salmonella.* This contamination spread into foods involving the use of egg products such as noodles and prepared cake mixes. Following FDA inspections, processors also recalled shipments of dried yeast, yeast tablets, and dried milk or products in which dried milk was used.

In one case, *Salmonella* was found in smoked fish that sickened more than four hundred people. FDA investigation showed that the fish-processing plant was contaminated.

The FDA has concluded that action must be taken to eliminate animal-based sources of infection, which result from contaminated feeds and feed mixes that use animal by-products. Feed additives such as processed fish meal, poultry meal, meat scraps, and meat meal are primary sources of *Salmonella.* These products have been processed without regard for sanitation because they were intended for animal consumption, and processors considered sanitation unnecessary. In 1967 the industry was warned that the FDA would regard as adulterated any animal by-product intended for animal feed where that by-product was found to be contaminated by *Salmonella*. Under the law, such material is subject to seizure.

One outbreak of salmonellosis, striking some three hundred people, resulted from contaminated eggs. Another involving more than five hundred persons was due to inadequate cooking and the mishandling of turkeys served at a banquet. Contaminated smoked ham was responsible for the illness of two people, and an outbreak affecting three others was traced to cake that had been contaminated by human carriers of the organism, who had handled the ingredients.

In 1964, after a world-wide increase in *Salmonella* food poisoning from egg products, the FDA began a preventive program aimed at dried and frozen eggs and foods containing eggs. The first action under the new program resulted from an outbreak of food poisoning among students in a Washington state college. State and local authorities, along with FDA inspectors, traced the cause to frozen eggs used in meringue pies prepared by a Spokane bakery. The eggs came from a Spokane commercial creamery that had never been licensed by the state to produce frozen eggs.

FDA inspectors located and sampled interstate shipments from the creamery, and court orders were obtained for the seizure of three lots in Montana. More than 420,000 pounds of frozen eggs from this firm were held up by the state. During the following ten months, samples were collected from

142 frozen and dried egg producers and food manufacturers using these products. Four seizures of contaminated frozen or dried eggs, and two seizures of commercial foods prepared from contaminated eggs, were made because they contained *Salmonella* organisms.

With the opening of the atomic age, FDA pioneered the monitoring of products to determine radioactivity levels. When atom-bomb tests were made in the Pacific, a Japanese fishing boat was exposed to radioactive fallout, and as a result the FDA undertook to examine all frozen tunafish that came from Japanese waters.

Later, in connection with its radioactivity studies, the FDA collected samples of raw agricultural food products, including animal fodders and forage. Roughly fifty different categories, including imported items (tea, coffee, cocoa beans, etc.) were analyzed for radioisotopes of primary interest—strontium-90, cesium-137 and iodine-131.

The FDA also conducted studies of market-basket samples of commodities recommended as a moderate-income diet for sixteen-to-nineteen-year-old boys—considered the country's biggest eaters. In this program, a two-week supply of food was bought from an eighty-two-item shopping guide, and was prepared in diet kitchens according to accepted home-cooking practices. The "total diet" included everything from soup to nuts, not forgetting hamburgers, hot dogs and soft drinks. Items were grouped in twelve major food categories, and composite samples were then tested in FDA laboratories for radioactivity. The food samples were taken from nine geographical areas, representing a good cross section of the United States.

Today radioactivity monitoring is carried on by the Public

Health Service, but it presents no great difficulties, since nuclear testing in the United States is done underground. However, the shopping-and-cooking "total diet" program of the FDA continues because it was ideally suited to testing for pesticide residues.

Pesticides are used today by the more than two million growers of fruits, vegetables, and other crops in the United States. In a single year these farmers used more than 175 million pounds of insecticides, in addition to large amounts of weed killers, fungicides and other poisons. More than five hundred basic chemicals are used in about sixty thousand registered pesticide products; and of these approximately three hundred chemicals are widely used in some forty thousand formulas.

All are important to farmers. The chemicals control insects, kill weeds, control plant diseases, stop fruit from dropping prematurely, make leaves fall so harvesting will be easier, make seeds sprout, keep seeds from rotting before they sprout, and have other uses aimed at improving the variety, quality and economy of the American food supply. Many of these chemical products, however, leave chemical residues on harvested crops, and without some form of safety precautions these residues could be extremely harmful to consumers of such crops.

Under the law, pesticide manufacturers must register their labels with the U. S. Department of Agriculture. The manufacturer must show that his pesticide will be: (a) effective in controlling the pests for which it is intended; and (b) safe for the user, other people, or animals in the area, and to other crops, when used as directed.

When pesticide labels recommend food-crop uses that will

leave residues, the FDA has the responsibility for seeing that the amount of the residues will be safe for consumers. Before the FDA acts to set a tolerance, the Department of Agriculture must certify to the FDA that the pesticide will be useful in agriculture, and specify what amount of residue will remain on the harvested crop. No tolerance is allowed for any substance that might produce cancer when consumed in small amounts for long periods.

FDA inspectors check to see that growers follow label directions or other reliable advice in the use of pesticides. They visit individual growers, talk with county agents, insect-control specialists and pesticide dealers, and review bulletins of agricultural authorities and pesticide manufacturers. In this way the inspectors learn what insect pests are giving trouble on what crops, what pesticides are being recommended, and where violations are most likely to occur.

Armed with this information, the inspectors collect samples of crops they think most likely to contain unauthorized residues, and they can tell laboratory scientists what to look for. The scientists are skilled in the techniques of detecting and measuring minute amounts of residue.

In the FDA laboratory is a gas chromatograph, a modern scientific instrument that can detect the amount of pesticides in parts *per billion*. Without this tool the FDA could not control the pesticide-residue problem as effectively as it does. Suppose an analysis has to be made of sample tomatoes that have been sprayed with one of forty different pesticides. If the FDA scientists had to apply forty different tests to single out the one pesticide, they would use up the samples. The gas chromatograph can make the identification with a single test. Although the device can't positively identify all pesti-

29

cides, it can pick out some sixty—virtually all of those that the FDA considers the most important and most toxic.

In addition to samples collected as a result of an inspector's investigation, other samples are taken strictly at random. The random samples show how well the farmers are complying with safety rules. Results show that the degree of compliance is very high. This is borne out by the "total diet" meals mentioned earlier, in which each individual food is examined for pesticide residue.

Most reputable food manufacturers cooperate with the FDA to stop distribution of contaminated foods. In fact the food industry voluntarily destroys thousands of tons of food, or diverts it to other (nonfood) use as the result of FDA inspections that show the food is unfit for human consumption.

The FDA says, "Food processors as a whole are aware of their responsibilities to maintain adequate sanitation controls in their factories. On each factory inspection, the FDA inspector invites the management to accompany him and learn firsthand the factors that FDA considers essential to good sanitation. At the end of the inspection he offers to discuss his observations, and leaves a written report of any conditions that might lead to violations. If the inspector collects investigational samples for filth analysis, a report of his findings is made to the firm."

Trouble from contaminated food is sometimes prevented at the source. For instance, the FDA may act to seize carloads of grain infested with insects or vermin, thus keeping the filthy grain from reaching the consumer. FDA educational programs designed to show growers and shippers how to keep commodities sanitary have been most productive. As the result of an FDA Grain Sanitation Program, about 75 percent of the total grain storage capacity of the United States was rebuilt to provide more sanitary handling of food grains.

Virtually any kind of food can become contaminated or otherwise harmful. The FDA has seized some products because they contained injurious substances; one, for example, was seized because it contained more than 0.1 milligrams of folic acid, which is the amount permitted in products not requiring a prescription. Folic acid has been known to mask symptoms of pernicious anemia when used in excessive quantities.

Unfortunately, illness or death sometimes result from carelessness or from the deliberate use of harmful materials in food processing. One such case occurred in the FDA's Philadelphia District.

Dale Kleinschmidt, three years old, of Haddon Heights, New Jersey, a Philadelphia suburb, died of food poisoning during Holy Week, the heart of the Lenten fast-and-fish season. Several members of the child's family became seriously ill, and three women who had eaten at a local restaurant had also taken sick. The boy, his family, and the women had all eaten fillet of flounder.

The FDA director assigned inspectors to talk with members of the dead boy's family, to doctors at Cooper Hospital where he died, the Haddon Heights police, employees of the Philadelphia restaurant where the women had dined, and health officials in Pennsylvania and New Jersey.

The inspectors reported that the little boy became ill soon after he ate the flounder. He began to turn blue and was a

31

very dark blue by the time he reached the hospital. Other members of the family had similar symptoms, as did the women who ate at the restaurant.

The child was dead upon arrival at the hospital. The resident doctor ordered all members of the family brought in for treatment. Not knowing the exact cause of the poisoning, he also telephoned the Philadelphia Poison Control Center and learned that the symptoms indicated chemical poisoning.

Members of the boy's family and the three women were given injections of methylene blue, and their symptoms began to fade. Their cases were diagnosed as sodium nitrite poisoning. Sodium nitrite is a poisonous chemical that reduces the ability of the red blood cells to carry oxygen through the body. The victim suffocates. The probable fatal dose for a 150-pound adult is from about a teaspoonful to an ounce.

The FDA inspectors learned that fish fillets and no other foods were involved in the poisoning. When they examined the fillets remaining at the restaurant and in the market where Dale's mother had bought the flounder, they found large quantities of the sodium nitrite.

Both lots of flounder had come from the same wholesale fish dealer in Philadelphia. Where else had the company shipped fish that might also be contaminated? Working against time, FDA men discovered that shipments from the same lot had been confined to a chain of food markets and the one restaurant. The chain-store deliveries did not go beyond southern and central New Jersey, upper Delaware and Pennsylvania points not more than fifty miles from Philadelphia.

Now the FDA alerted the Philadelphia Department of

Public Health, the New Jersey Health Department, and the office of the prosecutor in Camden County, New Jersey, all of whom had immediate access to radio, television and the press. Through these media, warnings were sent to the public not to touch flounder or fluke fillets bought but not yet eaten.

As usual, a flood of false rumors began. One was that the poisoned fillets came from New Bedford, Massachusetts. Others were equally wrong. Although the FDA had intended warnings to be local, the publicity resulted in a fourteen-state police teletype notice. Police cars in Washington used loudspeakers to blare warnings cautioning people not to eat flounder. Telephone calls came from worried men and women as far away as Boston and New Orleans.

Reports of more poisonings also poured in. Eventually 152 cases were recorded, but there was only one death beside that of the first small victim. The FDA assured the public that distribution of the poisoned fish had not gone beyond the area adjoining Philadelphia, and that all suspected fillets had been recalled and held. Panic subsided, but the official investigation went forward.

How had the sodium nitrite gotten into the fish? No nitrites may be used to preserve fish. But after a fish is filleted, it is common practice to clean it in a saline solution, usually a simple mixture of salt and water. Because sodium nitrite resembles ordinary table salt, FDA inspectors at first theorized that it might have been accidentally added to brine in which the flounder was cleaned.

The president of the seafood company that sold the fillets indignantly denied any use of sodium nitrite whatever. At the height of the scare, he appeared on a Philadelphia television program to declare that no one in the fish industry would deliberately use sodium nitrite. However, in his plant the inspectors found evidence of the poison under hoops on the brine barrels, on the concrete floor and on the company's cutting table. They knew that sodium nitrite could be used to "freshen" spoiled fish by removing its slime and bad smell, and their suspicions grew that the poison had been used deliberately for that purpose.

The FDA probe revealed that on several previous occasions the seafood company's customers had returned fish because it was decomposed. On Good Friday, three days after Dale Kleinschmidt's death, a persistent FDA inspector unearthed a record that nailed the company president. The inspector checked chemical and supply houses that sold sodium nitrite. At one of these he discovered that a "rush" delivery of four hundred pounds of the poison had been made to the seafood company the day before Dale died. He also learned that a smaller shipment had been delivered during Lent the year before.

The inspector established that the firm's president had personally authorized the latest order; more than that, he had actually accompanied the four-hundred-pound drum of sodium nitrite from the delivery truck to the room where the fish was being prepared.

All facts were presented to a grand jury, which indicted the seafood company, its president, and a foreman. The president was fined $2,500 and sentenced to serve one year in jail, but his attorney petitioned the court to release him because he suffered from heart trouble.

The seafood company soon went out of business, but the FDA and local health authorities made a nationwide investigation of domestic and imported fish and fish products. A few isolated cases of the use of sodium nitrite were unearthed, but in all of them the concentration of the poison was much lower than that used in Philadelphia. As a result of the survey, the FDA took all possible action to prevent tragedies such as that which took the life of three-year-old Dale Kleinschmidt.

Another deadly type of food poisoning is botulism, resulting from botulin bacteria growing in foods that have not been properly canned at home. Symptoms include vomiting, diarrhea, and an overall feeling of severe sickness and weakness. In many instances the disease is fatal.

One night an FDA inspector was doing his family's wash in a Washington, D. C., laundromat when he received a telephone call from his chief in Baltimore.

"There are four people in bad shape in the hospital here," the chief said. "They show all the symptoms of botulism, and we think the cause may be a meal they ate in Washington four days ago."

"Where? Do you know?" the inspector asked.

The chief gave him the name and address of a Washington woman who had entertained the ailing four at dinner. "Get on it right away, will you?" he said. "The hostess herself may need treatment, if she isn't getting it already."

The inspector left his wash with the manager of the laundromat. On the street he hailed a passing prowl car of the Washington Metropolitan Police Department, which sped to the home of the ex-hostess. The house was dark. The inspector rang the doorbell and pounded on the door until a light appeared. A tall, haggard-looking woman opened the door. She was startled to see police officers.

"What is it? What's the trouble?" she asked.

The inspector told her. "Have you been ill?" he asked. "How do you feel?"

"Not so good. My stomach keeps churning, and I've been doing some upchucking."

The inspector questioned her about the meals she served to her guests. She ticked off each dish. "And there was some okra," she said, "but there couldn't be anything wrong with that. I canned it myself."

That was the tip-off to the inspector. At his request the woman gave him a partly filled quart jar and an unopened pint jar of her okra. One sniff convinced him that the okra was the culprit. He persuaded the lady to dress and accompany him and the police officers to the hospital for treatment.

In the prowl car on the way, the inspector learned that the woman worked as a domestic, and that she had given two jars of her okra to one of her employers. She gave the inspector the employer's name and address. He left the sick woman at the hospital and rushed to the given address. There he discovered that the family had not yet eaten the canned okra but had sent one jar of it to a friend in Phoenix, Arizona. The inspector told the family about the poisoned food and took the jar.

A long-distance telephone call to Arizona prevented an attack of botulism in the home of the friend to whom the okra had been sent. All other jars of the suspected food were recovered before more of it was eaten.

The guests at the original dinner were not so lucky. Of the four in Baltimore, two died and two were saved by emergency treatment. The woman who had canned the okra was less seriously affected than any other victim—probably because she had consumed about a pint of castor oil the morning after the fateful dinner. However, doctors gave her botulin antitoxin, and she soon recovered completely.

At 2:30 A.M. the weary FDA inspector returned to the laundromat, picked up his wash, and trudged home.

On occasion a case such as the above might result in a brief local newspaper story, but there are countless FDA actions that are never publicized at all, because they occur without fanfare and are seldom sensational. They involve acts of *prevention*—doing away with hazards before serious harm is done.

One day, while walking through the processing area of a baby-food factory, an FDA inspector noticed an employee putting new nylon bristle brushes in one of two machines used to remove pits from peaches and to make the peaches into pulp. He noticed that the old brushes had about 90 percent of their bristles sheared from the wooden bases.

"How often are these brushes changed?" he asked.

"Usually about three times a day," the machine operator told him.

"Where do these pieces of nylon bristle go after they're sheared off in the machine? Not into the baby food, I hope."

"Oh, no, no. After the pulping stage, we have a fine-straining system that would keep the bristles from getting into the food."

The inspector, wanting to satisfy himself, took samples of the strained peaches to his district laboratory. Analysis there showed conclusively that there were specks of black nylon bristles in the baby food.

Back at the plant the inspector recommended corrective

action. The processors redesigned their equipment to eliminate completely the use of nylon brushes. Other manufacturers of baby foods were also advised to do away with the brushes, and took the advice. Today baby food contains no nylon bristle fragments.

Another story of prevention began on the wharves in New Orleans, Louisiana, where an FDA inspector was on his way to collect a sample of canned salmon from a ship that had just docked. On the pier he noticed another ship unloading hundred-pound bags of dried lima beans—six hundred bags in all, or sixty thousand pounds. A number of the bags were partly covered with a yellowish dust.

Nearby, he found a stack of small iron drums whose markings showed that they contained yellow oxide of lead. Questioning a shipping clerk, the inspector learned that the lima beans had been stowed in a lower hold of the same ship as the lead oxide.

"I see that some of the dust has settled on the bean sacks," the inspector said.

"Huh? Oh, yeah," the clerk answered, smiling. "When they unloaded the drums, one of the stevedores let one slip outa the sling. The drum busted, and that powder sifted over the beans."

"Did you report it?"

"Yeah, sure I did. If I didn't, we'd be one drum short."

"What about the beans?"

"What about 'em? None of them busted open. I ain't worried about the beans."

The FDA man took preliminary bean samples from four of the bags that showed the yellow dust. At the New Orleans FDA laboratory he rinsed the beans with diluted nitric acid and tested the washings. They showed a strong contamination with lead.

The next morning he returned to the wharf and collected an "official" sample of the beans. Then he arranged with New Orleans health authorities to order all six hundred bags embargoed.

At the FDA laboratory the chief chemist confirmed the inspector's preliminary analysis. There was high lead contamination in the beans. Consulting FDA consumer specialists, the inspector learned that cooks often add a little vinegar when boiling dried lima beans. Vinegar with lead oxide produces sugar of lead—a potent poison.

The New Orleans FDA district recommended that action be taken to seize the lot of contaminated beans. The recommendation was approved, and through the Department of Justice the seizure was made.

Soon the claim clerk for the steamship line showed up and asked, "How can we get our beans back?"

The FDA and the United States Attorney agreed to release the beans only if they could be made safe in compliance with the law. The company attempted to separate the bags showing the yellow dust from those that didn't appear to be contaminated. Then the FDA inspector took samples from the bags supposed to be safe. Laboratory analysis showed contamination, and the government refused to release any of the beans.

The company then arranged to put all the beans through a mechanical "bean cleaner." In this machine, clean sawdust and beans were tumbled together, then separated by sieving and winnowing. By this means the yellow oxide of lead was transferred from the beans to the sawdust, which was then destroyed. The old bags were burned and the cleaned beans were put into new sacks. Samples of all the cleaned beans showed them to be free of lead. They were then released and went into commercial channels as safe food.

But if it hadn't been for the keen eye of the conscientious FDA inspector, sixty thousand pounds of poisoned beans might have sent scores of people to hospitals—and some, perhaps, to their graves.

In the early days of enforcement of the food and drug laws, one source of trouble was the tomato industry. Conditions were deplorable. Refuse materials such as tomato peels, cores and other trimmings went into the making of tomato pulp and puree. The use of moldy, rotten tomatoes was common. The factories were filthy. Careless sorting and handling let decomposed material get into finished products that were marketed and found their way to kitchen tables.

R. J. Howard, who spent forty years (1902–1942) in the FDA, developed methods for detecting contamination in food and drug products and devised ways of analysis that put teeth into the government's campaign against filth and adulterants in food. Howard's attention was directed particularly to the tomato industry.

When he began his probe, there was no way in which wholesome, sound tomato products could be distinguished by laboratory analysis from products packed from moldy, rotten stock. Howard went to canneries and took pailfuls of tomatoes from conveyors just at the point where they were going into cooking kettles. He made naked-eye sortings of sound and rotten material to determine the percentage of rot. Then he examined under a microscope the canned product made from the groups of tomatoes from which he had taken samples. On a ruled slide he counted the number of areas that contained filaments of mold. By examining thousands of these matched pairs of samples, first with the naked eye, then with the microscope, he was able to set up a correlation between mold count and condition of the raw stock.

Through this method, Howard determined the point at which the mold count was positive proof that the product was unfit for human consumption and illegal. The validity of this so-called "Howard mold count" was upheld in court decisions and was generally accepted by the tomato industry.

Howard personally visited numerous tomato-processing factories in the United States and pointed out how their products could be improved. He also went to Italy and inspected over a hundred tomato-paste packing plants, suggesting improvements in sanitary conditions and packing methods.

Tomato packers today hire and train mold counters every season to run continuous checks to be sure that products such as catsup and tomato sauces are of good quality when they come off the assembly lines.

But commercial processors are not the only ones who should be health conscious. Simple precautions in the handling of food should also be taken in our homes to protect the health of our families. With this in mind, the FDA offers some helpful suggestions to housewives:

Keep hands, clothing, utensils, or anything that may touch food, scrupulously clean.

Keep animals and insects away from food.

Keep frozen foods frozen and perishable foods cold until you're ready to prepare them. Be sure cooked food doesn't stay long at room temperature either before or after serving.

If there is any doubt that leftover foods are fresh and good to eat, throw them away.

If a glass is broken near food, throw the food away rather than take a chance that it is safe to eat.

Remember that the food and drug laws are designed to protect us, the consumers. The least we can do is to read the labels and take Dr. Wiley's advice to judge for ourselves. Sometimes manufacturers cheat and labels lie, but eventually the FDA catches up with them. . . .

3

Laws and Labels

ON the wrapper of a loaf of bread you may find the words "calcium and sodium propionate added to retard spoilage." These are salts produced naturally in Swiss cheese, and they prevent bread from becoming moldy, especially in warm weather. In the bread they are food additives.

Food additives are any natural or synthetic substances added to foods to perform one or more specific functions. Modern food preparation is moving rapidly from the home kitchen to the food factory, and storage time is longer. We have "convenience" foods, heat-and-eat foods, ready-to-serve foods, food in pills and capsules, instant foods—even push-button foods.

Proper and safe additives are necessary to keep these and our other foods safe, pure, and wholesome. The Food, Drug, and Cosmetic Act of 1938 included a provision that made it unlawful to add any unsafe substance to food except where it could not be avoided. For unavoidable additives, the act provided that safe limits be set (as in the case of pesticides).

Food additives have many functions. For examples, spices and natural or synthetic flavors improve taste.

Starch, pectin, gelatin, gum arabic, agar and methyl cellulose are used to stabilize and thicken.

Quality production of many types of baked goods, soft drinks and candy requires additives to neutralize or alter acidity or alkalinity.

For ages people have used salt, sugar, vinegar, heat, freezing, smoke and spices to prevent or delay food spoilage. Modern science has developed preservatives such as sodium and calcium propionate to retard growth of bread molds and butylated hydrozytoluene (BHT) to retard oxidation that allows fats and fatty foods to become rancid.

Other additives retain moisture, add nutrients such as vitamins and minerals, mature and bleach flour, increase volume and smoothness, and act as propellants for food in pressurized cans.

Additives are also used for hardening, drying, coloring, leavening, antifoaming, noncaloric sweetening, disease prevention, creaming, firming, antisticking, whipping and sterilizing.

The FDA is responsible for establishing rigid safety standards for food additives. Not only must an additive be proved safe in normal use, but also safe when small amounts are consumed over a lifetime. Any additive could be harmful in some amount or under some circumstances. This is true even of such common additives as sugar and salt, which are quite safe in ordinary amounts for healthy people. The consumer should be interested in the safety of the amount allowed—he needn't be concerned about some larger amount than the FDA allows.

According to the FDA, "Many persons question modern additives because the additives don't yet have simple, common names, and because they aren't added in home cooking. But consumers should learn not to be alarmed by the word 'chemical'."

Proteins, fats, and carbohydrates are complex chemical compounds. In our kitchens we casually use such additives as salt, baking powder, vinegar, soda, cornstarch, cream of tartar and water, without thinking that we are actually using sodium chloride, calcium acid phosphate, acetic acid, sodium acid carbonate, amylum, potassium bitartrate and hydrogen oxide.

Allowable amounts vary according to types of food, the additive's safety, and the least amount needed to accomplish the desired result. For instance, the FDA allows BHT in dry cereals at the ratio of fifty parts per million. FDA scientists estimate that if BHT were used at the maximum level in all foods in which it is authorized, the maximum daily intake would be about four parts per million (4 ppm). Actual usage is substantially less. How much is four parts per million? Well, 4 ppm equals 128/1000 of one ounce for each ton of food; or, 4 ppm of all the food a person might eat in a normal lifetime would equal about four mouthfuls.

In 1960 the law was strengthened to bring food colors under the same kind of control that exists for other chemical food additives. The law covers all colors, and provides for tolerances and certification when necessary for safe use.

Also, foods must not be marketed if they are spoiled (putrid or decomposed) and must not be contaminated by insects, worms, rodent hairs, disease organisms, human or animal wastes, dirt, or poisonous substances. In addition, they must not be prepared, packed or stored under conditions that *might* contaminate them in any of these ways. Diseased animals, or animals that died from causes other than slaughtering, may not be used for foods.

Enforcing these food laws and regulations is no easy task. In some instances, while a food product itself may be clean when processing begins, individuals working in the plant may be a source of bacteriological contamination. Dirty hands can pass bacteria to the food or to the processing equipment, and FDA inspectors always check for the proper location of adequate hand-washing facilities. In some places they have found no washrooms at all. In others they have traced contamination to an all-purpose wipe cloth used by workers not only to dry their hands, but also to clean tabletops, utensils and machines.

Careful observation of time and temperature is of great importance in sanitary inspection. In one plant a batch of the base mix for chocolate cream pie was held for three days at room temperature. In addition to high germ counts there was a sizable growth of mold on the surface. Products made from this mix were seized.

In another plant a chop-suey mix was left at room temperature all day. The mix had been prepared the day before and stored overnight in shallow pans in a refrigerated room. When removed from the refrigerator, the mix had an aerobic plate count of 600 organisms per gram. (An aerobe is a microorganism that can live only in free air.) After sitting at room temperature until midmorning, the count was 1,500 per gram. By early afternoon two samples counted 320,000 and 660,000 per gram. The counts of the finished product, with packages placed in master cartons for blast-freezing, ranged from 5,000,000 to 10,000,000 bacteria per gram. The food was condemned, and a host of chop-suey eaters were saved from serious illness.

Racketeers have added to the FDA's enforcement problems—including incubator-reject egg racketeers. These operators collected infertile eggs rejected by hatcheries and trucked them to large plants where decomposed (rotten) eggs were broken out, frozen, and sold for use in food products. The whole operation, of course, was veiled in secrecy, making arrests and convictions difficult. One company in Jersey City, New Jersey, was convicted and fined $20,000, the maximum that could be imposed.

In another case the head of a cross-country incubator-reject racket was also a food processor. He was arrested and convicted, sentenced to a year in jail, put on probation for five years, and ordered to get out of the food business. Three of his accomplices were fined and placed on probation for five years.

The FDA says, "These cases are expected to help in breaking up this vicious practice, but the racket seems to be so lucrative that it will probably attract others."

Another important aspect of the food laws governs labeling. Food labels are required to be complete and correct. That is, the common or usual name of the food and of each ingredient must be stated. If a food contains two or more ingredients, they are listed in the order of predominance. For example, a blend of cane and maple syrup in which cane syrup predominates can't be called simply "Vermont syrup."

The label must state that the container holds "cane and maple syrups." If a can of tunafish and noodles has more noodles than tuna, "noodles" must be listed before "tuna" to avoid misleading consumers.

Many infractions of the food and drug laws involve improper labeling. In one 1967 case, counterfeit fish were seized in Salt Lake City, Utah. Packages labeled "halibut steaks" actually contained turbot, a European flatfish. Also, the FDA charged that the product was not a "steak" at all, but portions cut from a compressed block of fish particles.

A Fair Packaging and Labeling Act, which became effective July 1, 1967, provided additional means for the FDA to assure that foods, drugs, medical devices, and cosmetics are labeled honestly and informatively. FDA regulations issued under this Federal law say that "label" means any display of written, printed or graphic matter on the immediate container of any consumer commodity, or affixed to any such commodity or to any package containing a consumer commodity.

"Package" means any container or wrapping in which a consumer commodity is enclosed for delivery to retail buyers. Transparent wrappers that do not hide the required label information appearing on an inner label, and certain shipping or display containers, do not come within this definition.

"Principal display panel" of a food package means that part of a label that is most likely to be shown or examined under consumer conditions of display for retail sale.

"Area of the principal display panel" means the area of the side or surface of the package that bears the principal display panel.

Labels of food packages must carry: (1) a statement of the

identity of the food; (2) the name and address of the manufacturer, packer, or distributor; (3) a statement of the net quantity of the contents; (4) a statement of the net contents of a serving; and (5) a list of ingredients.

The statement of identity must appear on the principal display panel in bold type and in lines generally parallel to the base of the package as it is displayed. It shall be stated as the common or usual name of the food, such as "beets" or "peaches." If there is no common name, then appropriate descriptive terms or a commonly understood fanciful name may be used, such as trade names like Coca-Cola or Seven-Up. If a food is offered in various forms, such as whole, sliced or chopped, the particular form must be a prominent written part of the label, unless it is represented by a picture or when it can be seen through the container, such as a glass jar.

The statement of the net quantity must appear without any qualifying terms such as "giant quart" or "jumbo pound" that might exaggerate the amount of food in the package. The quantity must be in easily readable bold-faced type. If the product is liquid, the statement must be in terms of fluid measure—U. S. gallon, quart, pint or fluid ounce. If the food is solid, semisolid or viscous, or a mixture of solid and liquid, the label must show the weight in avoirdupois pounds and ounces. In the case of fresh fruits or vegetables, when sold by dry measure, the statement must be in terms of U. S. bushel, peck, dry quart, or dry pint.

If the label of any food package describes the content in terms of the number of servings, then it must also describe the size of each serving.

Imitations must be labeled as such—"imitation vanilla flavoring," for instance.

The food name must not be misleading. Bonito fish, for example, must not be labeled "tuna fish," and the terms "milk" or "whole milk" must not be used if part of the butter-fat has been skimmed off.

The FDA has made scores of seizures because of deceptive packaging. Foods seized included canned shrimp, oysters, tuna, peas and peaches that failed to comply with fill-of-container standards.

Substandard foods seized included low-fat butter; flaked tuna fish labeled "solid pack"; canned peaches with light syrup instead of heavy syrup as labeled; preserves with artificial color not permitted by the standard; margarine having fewer units of Vitamin A than declared on the label; cut green beans with stems; canned mushrooms labeled as containing butter but actually containing vegetable fat instead; tomatoes with excess peel; and noodles deficient in egg content.

Many seizures have been made of seafood containing items or varieties cheaper than those indicated by labels. Frozen shrimp, for example, contained fish, crabs, eels and seaweed, and "Maine Lobster Newburg" turned out to be artificially colored scallops.

Imitation sorghum, butterscotch chips and cherry cider were seized because they were labeled as genuine.

A blend labeled "olive, peanut and corn oils" was seized because cottonseed oil had been substituted. A lemon powder was seized because it was an imitation of dehydrated lemon juice. One brand of syrup claimed to be a blend of 85 percent cane and 15 percent maple, but had undeclared imitation maple flavor. "Banana tea cookies" contained no bananas, and "fancy genuine Italian grated cheese" was a domestic product.

Debased products seized have included lemon extract deficient in lemon oil and ethyl alcohol, bulk wheat containing oats, a bakery-pan coating containing mineral oil instead of vegetable oil, frozen oysters with excessive water and "Swiss cheese" with artificial holes that made it appear of greater value.

The foregoing labeling requirements do *not* apply to "standardized foods." Just as we have legal reference standards to insure uniformity in weights and measures, so do we have legal reference standards to insure the composition and quality of many of our basic foods.

How do we know that the jar of "strawberry preserves" we bought at the market is really strawberry preserves and not a mixture of water, pectin, artificial coloring, artificial flavoring, and grass seed? How different can two brands of tomato catsup be and still be truthfully labeled "tomato catsup"? How do we know that canned "early June peas" won't be so hard and mealy as to be inferior in quality, or that canned "whole peaches" will be uniform in size and color and free from blemishes?

Food standards give us the assurance we need. There are three kinds of standards—identity, quality, and fill. In general, standards are for identity. These prevent adulteration by defining what a food should contain—what the consumer is entitled to receive when he purchases the food by its common or usual name. For example, fruit jams must contain 45 parts of fruit and 55 parts of sugar or other sweetener; and raisin bread must have raisins equaling 50 percent of the weight of the flour.

Manufacturers who want to enrich certain foods must follow requirements in FDA's standards for "enriched" foods. These standards specify what foods may be enriched, what vitamins and minerals may be added, and in what amounts. Such staples as bread, flour, cornmeal, rice, margarine and evaporated milk are among those so labeled.

Standards of quality set minimum specifications for such factors as tenderness, color, and freedom from defects in canned fruits and vegetables. Quality standards for canned foods limit the "string" in green beans, excessive peel in tomatoes, hardness in peas, "soupiness" in cream-style corn and pits in pitted canned cherries.

Standards of quality should not be confused with Grades A, B, C, Prime, Choice, Fancy and so on, which are set by the U. S. Department of Agriculture (USDA). Manufacturers pay USDA for this voluntary service. Impartial USDA graders rate meats, canned goods, and other products for quality—but regardless of its USDA grade, any food sold in the stores is wholesome, due to FDA's standards and efforts.

Standards of fill tell the packer how full a container must be to avoid deceiving the consumer and to avoid charges of "slack filling."

Under the law, not all standardized foods are required to have *all* ingredients listed on labels. The standard defines what the food must contain, and the name of the food tells the consumer what it is. In certain cases the standard itself may require some or all of the ingredients to be listed, if this is determined to be in the interest of the consumer. Artificial colors and flavors, and chemical preservatives, must be declared on the labels of all foods containing them, except butter, cheese, and ice cream. Nonstandardized foods must bear a complete list of their ingredients.

Products with false or misleading labeling are "misbranded." Federal law prohibits the shipment of misbranded products across state lines. Labels that are literally true have been held to be misleading because of what they failed to tell the buyer, or because the product was not what the consumer expected when he selected it by its common or usual name.

The law also prohibits shipment of "adulterated" products. The presence of any harmful, spoiled or filthy material is prohibited. Adulteration includes all kinds of cheating in foods, such as adding starch to cocoa, leaving vitamins out of enriched bread or substituting water for fruit juice.

One of the more important food fraud cases investigated by the FDA involved a company that was adding water and sugar to its "Fresh Orange Juice As Nature Made It."

FDA inspectors were sure that the Cal-Tex Company of Houston, Texas, was watering and sweetening its orange juice to reap fraudulent profits estimated at a million dollars annually, but for more than a year the FDA investigators had been unable to get direct evidence showing how and when the water and sugar were added.

In three separate inspections of the plant, inspectors found no sugar and no illegal operations. They found only pure orange juice entering the tanks, but laboratory analyses of samples taken from the liquid already in the tanks showed heavy adulteration.

After the second inspection the FDA inspectors concluded that when they arrived at the plant, the blending tank already contained the adulterated product, but that during the inspection only pure orange juice flowed into the tank. If that were true, an interval sampling of the tank after their arrival should show adulterated juice gradually becoming purer.

The hunch paid off. As soon as they arrived for the third inspection at 8:15 A.M. one morning in March, they took samples and continued to take additional samples from the tank at intervals until 10:45 A.M. During that time only pure orange juice went into the tank. Chemical analyses of the periodic samples showed a steady buildup of the pure content from about one half orange juice at 8:15 to nearly full strength at 10:45.

The FDA then took samples of interstate shipments of the firm's product and seized a tank carload of adulterated juice consigned to a subsidiary in Missouri. The firm did not contest the seizure, and the Federal court in Houston granted a government request for a temporary restraining order. However, at a later hearing the court refused to issue an injunction forbidding the company to make further shipments. Company officials stoutly contended that their product was pure, but said it was subject to variations such as occur in all natural products. The judge accepted their word.

This was a serious setback for the FDA. It meant that Cal-Tex could continue to adulterate its product and market it at a lower competitive price. Such a situation might result in the industry-wide watering of orange juice.

FDA investigators checked wholesalers in the hope of finding sources from which the company bought sugar, but the effort was fruitless. Either Cal-Tex was buying sugar under another name or was getting it from dealers in other cities.

There was one other way to find the answer. If the investigators could keep the processing plant under observation, they should be able to see if and when deliveries of sugar were made.

The FDA men rented a small apartment nearby, from which they could see the rear yard of the plant. The men were equipped with binoculars, a motion picture camera and a still camera with a telephoto lens.

For ten hot July days the inspectors watched the orange-juice plant. On each day they saw ten to twenty sacks of sugar unloaded from an unmarked green panel truck in the yard—but the sacks weren't taken into the plant. Instead, they were carried to another building in the rear. With their telephoto lens the inspectors were able to identify the markings on the bags.

The inspectors also saw an almost continuous "bucket brigade"—employees emerging from the back door of the plant with an empty bucket in each hand, walking across the yard to the rear building and returning with full pails of a "white powder" (sugar). Still photographs and movies recorded the whole operation.

The FDA men also saw periodic deliveries of barrels of corn syrup and were able to get photographs showing the brand name. They noted that the volume of fresh oranges entering the plant during their ten watchful days, and the amount of peel removed, were small in relation to the volume of finished orange juice being produced.

Armed with their evidence, the FDA men obtained a search-and-seizure warrant. While one team watched from the apartment, two other inspectors and a deputy U. S. marshal entered the plant with the warrant. They were delayed in the main office for some ten minutes—as had happened during earlier inspections. This time the inspectors in the apartment could see what went on during the delay. A buzzer sounded at the rear of the plant. Instantly the yard became alive. Men ran to the rear building and were seen moving boxes about. At the plant building, the machine that had been ejecting small quantities of orange peel suddenly spun into frantic action, and in just a few minutes the orange skins filled a waiting truck and spilled over to the ground.

When the inspectors and marshal entered the juice plant, they found a partially filled barrel of corn syrup, but there was no sugar anywhere.

They went quickly to the rear building, which seemed to house only cases of orange juice, some of them stacked to the ceiling along one wall. No sugar was in sight. Then one of the inspectors heard a gritty sound as he walked past the cases—the kind of noise that comes from stepping on sugar or salt. He removed some of the stacked cases and discovered that they were not against the wall, as they appeared to be, but were far enough from it to leave space where sacks of sugar were hidden.

Analyses of orange-juice samples prepared for shipment showed not only that the juice had been watered, but also that it contained sugar and commercial glucose. The glucose reflected an attempt to conceal a high percentage of sucrose in the adulterated product. The processors did not know that the FDA had a specific test for finding commercial glucose. The FDA analysis also showed a Vitamin C content higher than average, indicating that the vitamin was added to cover up the fact that the juice was deficient in this natural ingredient.

Later investigation established that the sugar, corn syrup, and Vitamin C were bought with cash as needed. When all the facts were in, it was apparent that the firm's annual cheat was close to one million dollars.

The company officials were indicted in Houston for conspiring to violate the Food, Drug, and Cosmetic Act, but legal maneuvering by the defense delayed a trial for eighteen months. The FDA took advantage of this delay to strengthen its evidence.

An apparent weak point in FDA's data on the composition of orange juice was a relative lack of information about Texas-grown oranges. Most of the laboratory work on the composition of orange juice for fifty years had been done on Florida and California fruit. While awaiting the trial, the FDA examined thousands of Texas oranges of different varieties from different groves during two growing seasons. They established that Texas oranges are not materially different from those grown in Florida and California—and this prevented the defense from claiming that FDA's facts could not apply to Texas oranges.

The FDA also worked out proof that Houston city water, which is naturally high in fluoride content, had been used to water the Cal-Tex orange juice.

The defendants were convicted of conspiracy, but the conviction was reversed by an appellate court on the grounds that the indictment was not properly drawn and did not sufficiently define the offense charged. Later, however, three of the company officials pleaded guilty to a charge of misbranding sweetened, watered orange juice sold in place of pure orange juice. Each received a $2,000 fine, a suspended one-year prison term, and five years probation. The president of the trucking firm servicing the company was fined $1,000 and also placed on probation for five years.

More mystifying than watered orange juice was a food-fraud conspiracy involving an adulterated vanilla extract. Under chemical analysis the extract showed up as the real thing, yet everyone concerned knew there was something wrong with it.

The Plantation Extract Corporation was organized in 1935 by a chemist and pharmacist who pooled their special skills to produce the fake vanilla extract and other adulterated flavorings. By 1940, Plantation was the nation's largest producer of so-called pure vanilla extract, and had a virtual monopoly on government and institutional business. More and more it took trade away from competitors, often bidding prices below the cost of the vanilla beans and alcohol needed to make legitimate vanilla extract.

Urgent complaints from competing firms set off an early FDA investigation. But repeated inspections of the firm and chemical analyses of its vanilla extract failed to solve the riddle. The analyses showed that the vanilla met government specifications and the generally accepted standard of vanilla extract. Although the product wasn't considered high grade in flavor, government agencies accepted it because Plantation was the lowest bidder, and specifications were apparently being met.

An intensive FDA investigation turned up an amazing story. First: How could a company make an adulterated vanilla extract that would show up as pure? Answer: by using St.-John's-wort, a weed whose resins are normally not distinguishable from those of vanilla extract. The company made an extract of St.-John's-wort in the same way an extract of vanilla was prepared. It was brown, bitter, and had none of the flavor characteristics of vanilla. It had one appealing feature—it cost about six cents a pound, compared to about eleven dollars a pound for vanilla beans. Plantation's "pure vanilla extract" consisted of a mixture in about equal parts of genuine vanilla extract and extract of St.-John's-wort. To overcome the latter's bitter taste, the makers added sugar syrup, then used synthetic vanillin to build up the vanillin content to the normal amount for pure vanilla extract.

The company's formula came from the chief chemist in the Food Subsistence Laboratory at the Army General Depot in New York, who "rendered services" to Plantation for a price. An authority on the composition and analysis of pure vanilla extract, he provided a recipe for an adulterated extract that would allow a high margin of profit and also escape detection.

In addition, this man insured against the Army's rejection of Plantation's vanilla. He set himself up as an expert on vanilla extract, and notified all other army food laboratories that certain brands of vanilla could be accepted for purchase, while other brands should be viewed with suspicion. All of Plantation's brands were on the list of "pure" products.

The vanilla fraud became so profitable and successful that Plantation branched out into other products—"pure lemon extract," sold to the Army and government agencies, and to the general trade; "imitation vanilla flavor," "nonalcoholic lemon flavor," and "nonalcoholic orange flavor," sold to the Navy; and "breakfast cocoa," sold to the Army and Navy.

All of these products were seriously manipulated with cheap and inferior materials, but unlike the fake vanilla, their adulteration could be detected easily. The scheme was sure to fail unless individuals in key positions in the Army and Navy could be "reached."

The key chemist in the Army's food laboratory furnished

needed protection for deliveries to the Army, but he was also instrumental in bringing in a civilian inspector who had a strategic position with the Navy Food Laboratory in Brooklyn. In his job, this civilian received, from deliveries made to navy posts, all samples of food taken by navy inspectors throughout the country. He entered the samples in his book, assigned numbers to them, and delivered them to the food laboratory for analyses. A scheme was worked out so that he then switched good proof samples for adulterated samples taken from deliveries of Plantation products around the country. Thus, while grossly adulterated flavors and cocoa were being delivered to Navy posts, the Brooklyn laboratory reported the products to be in full compliance with Navy specifications.

As Plantation's business grew to monopoly proportions, the conspirators had to figure out how to allay growing suspicions in the trade and government. They went to large and reputable wholesale grocery houses throughout the nation that did business with the government, and persuaded them to enter into working arrangements whereby they would, in effect, serve as fronts for Plantation.

These firms would bid for government business, and if awarded contracts, Plantation would manufacture, bottle, label and ship the products in the name of the contracting firm direct to government posts. The collaborating firms would submit bids on direction of Plantation without knowing that other bidders had similar arrangements. Frequently Plantation would dictate a different price to be quoted by each of the firms and would switch the award to the chosen firm by having it quote the lowest price. Where no collaborating firm was bidding, Plantation itself would bid sufficiently low to get the contract. With this scheme, Plantation got all the government business without appearing to get more than a normal share.

FDA investigators uncovered the whole story, and the conspirators were indicted and brought to trial in 1943. Two trials were necessary before they were brought to justice.

Even the trials had aspects of detective fiction. Final conviction hinged on FDA ability to show that Plantation's vanilla extract contained St.-John's-wort—whose resins were supposedly indistinguishable from those of pure vanilla extract. Through exhaustive research, FDA scientists were able to isolate from St.-John's-wort a red pigment that does not appear in vanilla resins. In a dramatic courtroom climax, an FDA chemist demonstrated this until-then-unknown difference in the two resins. The testimony of expert witnesses for the defense was thereby discredited, and the FDA won the case.

As shown by this and many similar cases, the FDA tries hard to keep harmful or fraudulent substances from getting inside our bodies—but what about the outside? Another area of potential danger involves cosmetics. Beauty is a big business in the United States today, with retail cosmetic sales approaching three billion dollars a year.

In California, one woman and her husband had worked hard for several years to build up their restaurant business, in which the woman served as hostess-manager. Conscious of the premium our society places on youth and beauty, she was fearful that an aging appearance would be detrimental in her work, and was attracted by certain advertisements that promised face-lifting without surgery. She fell for the lure, and the carbolic acid that was applied to her face disfigured her horribly for life. She sued, but in vain, for the practitioner had moved and created a new corporation in another state.

The Food and Drug Act of 1906 had no provisions for public protection from harmful cosmetics, and many consumers were seriously injured by unregulated beauty preparations. The passage of the 1938 Food, Drug and Cosmetic Act was largely hastened because of the use of dangerous chemicals in hair and eyebrow preparations, eyelash colors, and skin bleaches.

A cosmetic, as defined in the 1938 law, is an article (except soap) used for cleansing, beautifying, promoting attractiveness or altering the appearance of the human body; also articles intended for use as components of such products. Hormone creams, skin bleaches and certain types of deodorants are also classed as drugs under the law.

A cosmetic that is harmful under conditions of use, or that is falsely labeled, is subject to court action. One such case involved "cinnamon hot toothpicks" which contained cinnemaldehyde, a poisonous substance.

Colors used in cosmetics (except hair dyes, which have special labeling requirements) must be proved safe. Besides stating the net weight, a cosmetic label must tell the truth. One blue-colored shampoo had all required information on its label—but the printing was on the reverse side and could not be read until most of the shampoo had been used. The product was seized.

Special consumer protection information must be given on the labels of coal-tar hair dyes. Some of the coloring materials used in such dyes are known to cause allergic reactions—

redness, itching, blistering or swelling of the skin in some persons. Sometimes the reactions are temporarily disabling. To protect these persons, the law requires that any hair-dye product known to produce allergic reactions must carry on the label a conspicuous warning that its use may cause skin irritation and that a sensitivity test, called a "patch test," should be made before each use. The label must also warn that the use of these colors on eyelashes or eyebrows may cause blindness.

Labeling requirements for cosmetic-type preparations that are classed as "drugs" under the law are the same as for other drugs.

The FDA has taken the position that cosmetics used to color parts of the body, such as lipstick, rouge, nail enamel, eye shadow and mascara, are classified as "color additives" and must be shown safe for their intended use before they may be marketed. Certain manufacturers have contested this interpretation of the law.

Products intended for removing wrinkles or growing hair are drugs which must meet the more stringent drug provisions of the law. Wrinkle removers, for instance, have been involved in seizure actions on charges that they are "new drugs" and have not been proved safe and effective for the conditions for which they were promoted.

Unfortunately, the law doesn't require that cosmetics generally be proved safe before they go on the market, or that their ingredients be listed on labels. Also, the composition of a product may be changed from time to time, though sold under the same label. Since many manufacturers want to keep cosmetic formulas secret, the FDA must make extensive and time-consuming special analyses to identify various in-

gredients. The entire analytical problem is made more difficult by the perfumes that are present in all but a small frac-
tion of cosmetics. Perfumes are widely suspected by the medical profession to be the cause of many reactions.

In recent years there have been widespread seizures of hair
lacquer pads, shampoos that caused eye irritation and press-on
nail covers. Quantities of the press-on nail covers were recalled after many consumers discovered that removal of the
covers also removed the original nails! Nail undercoatings
and cold-wave neutralizers have also been the subject of
large-scale recalls.

In cosmetics, foods, drug or devices, everything the FDA
does is aimed at protecting the consumer. It has a Consumer
Services Staff that develops and distributes materials to give
families enough background knowledge to read labels so
they can buy foods intelligently, use drugs safely and effectively and protect their members from harm.

The FDA also has a staff of consumer specialists working
out of its eighteen district offices across the nation. These experts can provide informational materials, make helpful talks,
give demonstrations and exhibits to civic clubs, church organizations, youth groups and senior citizens. In one year,
for instance, they made more than a thousand speeches, arranged more than twelve hundred exhibits, made nearly three
hundred radio broadcasts and one hundred television appear-
ances, and took part in a hundred public or professional panel
discussions.

The FDA produces teachers' guides and student material
on foods, drugs, and cosmetics for use in schools. Some of the
student pamphlets have interesting titles, such as "Citizen-

ship and the Strawberry Jam," "How Safe Is Our Food?," "The Protection of Human Life" and "Young Scientists Look at Food." As this book was being written, the FDA was preparing booklets on drugs for the use of teachers or leaders of youth groups. Information concerning these materials may be obtained by writing to the Educational Services Staff, Food and Drug Administration, 200 C Street, S. W., Washington, D. C. 20204.

Despite such educational activity, many consumers continue to fall prey to health quacks—unscrupulous people who promote deceptive food fads and engage in other nutritional trickery.

4_____

The Health Quacks

YOU can't believe everything you read—even on some food labels.

A Detroit, Michigan, firm shipped quantities of canned fruit-type drinks into Indiana and Kentucky. The drinks supposedly had health value because they allegedly contained specified amounts of Vitamin C (ascorbic acid). FDA examination of samples showed that "shortages varied from 30 to 100 percent of the 30 mg. of Vitamin C declared per 6 fluid ounces." Seizure was made of 548 cases.

In New York City a Federal grand jury indicted the promoters of certain safflower-oil capsules, together with a medical doctor who wrote a book mentioning the advantages of safflower-seed oil and vitamins in weight reduction. The book named the New York firm that distributed the safflower-oil capsules. The book, label, box and an insert with the capsules said that a person could consume thousands of calories daily without regard to his total caloric intake, so long as he ate a high fat diet and took the capsules. The indictment charged postal fraud, conspiracy and food and drug violations. The food and drug counts charged "intent to defraud and mislead." According to the FDA, "The capsules are worthless in obesity control."

Members of the firm pleaded guilty to misdemeanors, were fined and given suspended sentences. The physician-author was fined $7,000, given a suspended sentence of two years and placed on probation for two years. He planned to appeal the verdict. After the indictment, more than five million safflower-oil capsules were recalled and destroyed by the manufacturer.

In the field of nutrition the law prohibits deceptive and misleading claims in labeling. Says the FDA, "This type of promotion has been called 'nutritional quackery' and has been estimated to cost American consumers as much as 500 million dollars a year. This estimate is believed conservative."

In the Food, Drug and Cosmetic Act, Congress recognized that the American shopper has the right to be fully informed about the nutritional value of foods he buys at the grocery store. The 1938 law took notice of the fact that certain foods were promoted for their special nutrient content, such as vitamins and minerals that were just coming into use as food additives. Besides requiring informative labeling, the law provided for the setting of standards for many common food items so that the average housewife could be sure that a product contained the ingredients she expected. In many instances these requirements applied to nutritional health products such as "enriched" flour—flour with added thiamin (Vitamin B^1), riboflavin (Vitamin B^2), niacin and iron.

The FDA regulations governing labeling of special dietary foods include foods claimed to have special value for vitamin and mineral content, those for use in low-sodium diets, weight-control diets, sugar-restricted diets and baby formula preparations.

Although our food supply is abundant and has high nutritional quality, consumers are constantly bombarded by exaggerated claims made by food faddists, nutritional quacks and even by many otherwise ethical food manufacturers. Consumers have become conscious of many terms they don't understand, such as "high quality" as applied to protein; "polyunsaturated," "unhydrogenated," "enzymes," "low calorie—more nutritive" and the like. Many look for these terms on labels in a misguided effort to protect the health of their families.

The FDA says these people are wasting an estimated half billion dollars a year on dietary items they don't need. In some cases the purchasers are from low-income groups who need the money for groceries and medical care. Some are elderly people living on low retirement benefits. They suffer more than any other age group from the chronic diseases that are particularly stressed by the promoters of special dietary items who claim their products will ward off or cure anything from memory defects to strokes, diabetes and cancer.

In the wake of advances in nutritional science, some firms have deliberately misinterpreted findings and exploited them for private gain. According to the FDA, "They employ clever copywriters to promote products by pseudoscientific statements using half-truths, innuendo and gross exaggeration to build up a scare psychology that will persuade people to buy nutritional supplements and other special foods, whether or not they actually need them. This type of nutritional quackery is both an economic and a health problem, since unsuspecting individuals may rely on self-diagnosis and ineffective treatment of serious illnesses."

According to the FDA, the American public's most serious nutritional problem is excess weight due to overeating, and promoters of dietary specialties haven't missed the opportunity to offer gullible buyers various schemes purporting to enable one to lose pounds without dieting. The label of one dietary food supplement promised that it was effective for removing pounds and inches in eight hours, and that one had to diet for only one meal a day and could eat normally otherwise without counting calories.

One case involved "weight reducing" and "appetite suppressant" capsules containing phenylpropanolamine (PPA for short). The manufacturer produced and marketed the capsules under numerous brand names. The government showed by extensive clinical and animal studies that 75 milligrams of PPA per day, as recommended by the makers, would not control weight. One of the brands, Unitrol, carried on the label the words, "Unitrol—That's All." *Inside* each bottle of capsules was a 1,180-calorie diet chart, with a statement that in order to lose weight, one's caloric intake must be reduced and certain types of food avoided. A Federal judge ruled that the products were useless for reducing weight and that the label statement, "Unitrol—That's All," was misleading because the prospective purchaser was given no hint at the time he bought the capsules that he must diet to lose pounds.

Another product with misleading comparisons of food values was a "tonic" for the prevention of anemia, which claimed to contain in one bottle as much essential iron as forty pints of raw oysters, ninety-three pounds of spinach, or sixty pounds of fish.

FDA inspectors and laboratory scientists have found that "for the most part" the label *potency* claims for special dietary foods reflect fairly accurately the amounts of the various nutrients in the products. Claims for the *usefulness* of the product, however, are frequently grossly distorted and exaggerated.

In one case the FDA brought criminal and injunction actions against a dentist who promoted more than 115 so-called nutritional products for treatment of more than five hundred different diseases and conditions.

In another, the seizure of numerous lots of vitamin and mineral food supplements, nationally promoted through door-to-door peddling, resulted in the destruction of many tons of false and misleading promotional material and in putting the company out of business.

While some vitamins may be taken in large amounts without harm, there are others whose excessive use may be hazardous. In 1964 a question was raised by a prominent physician concerning possible danger from the excessive use of Vitamin D by pregnant women and by infants. After a thorough study by scientists in the FDA, by the Committee on Nutrition of the American Academy of Pediatrics, and the Council on Foods and Nutrition of the American Medical Association, a proposed regulation was published limiting the amount of Vitamin D that could be present in ordinary food items.

Evaluation of claims made in labeling of foods promoted for nutritional health, and the enforcement of regulations requiring truthfulness of the potency declarations, must be based on facts revealed by laboratory investigations. FDA's Division of Nutrition conducts research in nutrition, metabolism and physiology. Also, chemical and biological studies are made to develop fast analytical methods for examining samples to determine nutrients and their biological availability in foods and feeds.

The availability to the body of vitamins or other nutrients is a recurrent problem under continuing study. Chemical analysis of some tablets may show the proper quantities of labeled *active* ingredients, but because of *inert* substances used to give preparations a suitable form or pleasant taste, or because of the nutrient form, or failure of the tablet to disintegrate, or, in the case of liquids, their dispersion in body fluids, the nutrients may not be released for maximum benefit.

The educational campaign against nutritional quackery has both a positive and negative side. In the positive approach the FDA uses its own sources of nutrition information and those of other agencies, particularly the Public Health Service and the Department of Agriculture. The negative approach involves a continuing effort to debunk quackery and its spurious claims and products.

Elderly and middle-aged men and women are often the main targets exploited by the nutritional and medical quacks. Senator Harrison A. Williams, in a report to the Senate Special Committee on Aging concerning frauds and deceptions affecting the elderly, said, "To the unscrupulous, the retirement-age group has several new and irresistible attractions. Buying power is one. Elderly Americans, about eighteen million in all, have an annual income of about thirty-seven billion dollars. It comes in the form of Social Security payments, pension plans, returns from savings and investments and part-time or full-time employment."

The senator pointed out that the incomes of many older people are pitifully inadequate and cause considerable worry about shelter, health care and protection against financial crises. "Anxiety," he said, "is thus a weapon for those who cheat the elderly, and so is the complexity of the modern marketplace. On every side, the elderly—and all other consumers—are confronted with claims made for products that can be evaluated only by experts. . . . Our older citizens have become a clearly defined market, not only for reputable businessmen with new and valuable products for the elderly, but also to those who are looking for a vast new market to victimize."

A great many older men and women suffer from some type of chronic condition such as cancer, rheumatoid arthritis, heart disease or diabetes. These are the people who are most cheated by the medical confidence man and the nutritional quack.

Seizures have been made of soybean lecithin promoted for digesting fats, particularly for people over forty; also for this age group, amino acids to fight diseases and infections, fortify heart and brain tissues and produce enzymes and hormones. The labels of both products bore misleading claims that the nutritional requirements of older people are different from those of adults generally. Vitamin products have been seized for claims that they will strengthen vision and brain, prevent rheumatic pains, hardening of the arteries, asthma and infections of mucous membranes.

One company in Chicago, Illinois, was charged with falsely promoting certain "capsulets" as a vitamin-mineral supplement to prevent worry, tension, lack of energy and depression. The same company made and sold tablets said to bring twenty-four-hour relief from neuralgia, lumbago, arthritis and stiff joints. The FDA seized the tablets and the capsulets on charges that they were misbranded by "false and misleading claims."

Many people, especially the elderly, are cautioned by their doctors to eliminate salt from their diets. One Utah dairy firm produced what it said was "salt-free Swiss cheese," but the FDA said that the cheese contained 24 milligrams of sodium (salt) per 100 grams of cheese, and the product was seized.

Certain "dietary supplement tablets" made by a Vermont company were seized because they were 40 percent deficient in the amount of Vitamin A the label claimed they contained.

A Chicago manufacturer marketed a beef tea which was seized by the FDA because of "false and misleading claims to reduce blood lipids [organic substances insoluble in water, including fats and waxes], reduce body weight, prevent cancer, diabetes, artery disease and heart attacks."

Seizure of multivitamin tablets, vitamin mineral tablets and protein wafers in California followed an FDA charge that all were deficient in Vitamin C.

One important milestone on the FDA's rocky road to health protection involved claims made for an appetite-control and weight reduction product called Regimen Tablets. The tablets were nationally advertised as being effective to reduce weight without drastic diet changes. The sponsors promised that the pills would cause a weight loss of 6½ pounds in seven days, would satisfy hunger and suppress appetite, letting pounds and inches melt away, and that they were made of a combination of reducing drugs so amazing that weight would vanish while the Regimen consumer continued to eat his favorite foods, including desserts and potatoes. In addition, the sponsors claimed that Regimen had been proved amazingly effective in clinical tests on overweight people, and that the weight loss would be permanent. They also said that fat people had been shown to be more susceptible to cancer than others.

One of the basic ingredients of Regimen Tablets was phenylpropanolamine. In large doses, said the FDA, this might cut one's appetite, but any quantity large enough to do this might be dangerous and should be taken only by prescription under a doctor's orders. The amount included in such over-the-counter drugs as Regimen isn't enough to cut appetite effectively. The tablets also contained ammonium chloride and benzocaine.

On February 13, 1962, U. S. marshals seized a quantity of the "three-way-drug combination" (green, yellow and pink tablets) in Denver, Colorado. The FDA, in this seizure action, challenged the claims made for Regimen Tablets, which were distributed by the Drug Research Corporation in New York. The FDA further asserted that the claims appeared in newspaper advertisements sponsored by that company, and that one of these ads was displayed with Regimen Tablets at the point of sale, which constituted "labeling." In other words, the claim was that Regimen was misbranded and was in interstate commerce, which brought it under the Food,

Drug and Cosmetic Act. The seizure action was transferred to Brooklyn, New York, for trial.

The president and chief stockholder of the Drug Research Corporation of New York was John T. Andreadis, also known as John Andre. According to the FDA, Andreadis had been promoting weight-reducing preparations since about January 1, 1947. Initially, promotion and distribution were by mail order only. Over the years, the Post Office Department had issued several orders charging him with using the mails to defraud. Following each fraud order, Andreadis would go out of business, then start again with a product and company of a different name. For a time, around 1957, the Wonder Drug Company sold Regimen by mail, but again the Post Office issued a fraud order.

Andreadis then started to distribute the product through retail stores and backed it up with an extensive national campaign in magazines, newspapers and on television. The claims were the same: Lose twenty-five to thirty pounds in thirty days, without dieting or eating special foods.

As complaints began to come in from Better Business Bureaus, various state agencies, the Post Office Department, the Federal Trade Commission and other bodies, the advertising media demanded that Andreadis produce clinical proof of Regimen's extravagant claims.

Andreadis complied with these demands through an attorney, Arthur D. Herrick, who had set up the New Drug Institute. Alleged clinical tests were submitted to, and accepted by, the advertising agency of Kastor, Hilton, Chesley, Clifford and Atherton, Inc. (Later testimony of former employees of the agency indicated that the agency was aware that Regimen couldn't possibly produce weight loss without dieting.)

Andreadis and his Drug Research Corporation contested the seizure of Regimen Tablets at Denver, but withdrew their opposition when overwhelming evidence at the seizure trial showed that the "clinical tests" were faked.

Andreadis agreed to a court order permanently prohibiting further distribution of Regimen Tablets with claims for weight control, and authorized the FDA to destroy all seized pills. This marked the beginning of many seizures of Regimen Tablets to remove them from the nationwide market.

In December, 1963, the United States attorney presented an indictment of fifty-eight counts to a Federal grand jury in Brooklyn, charging mail fraud, wire fraud, conspiracy to defraud and violation of the Food, Drug and Cosmetic Act. The indictment resulted directly from an FDA investigation following the Denver seizure, and no other agency took part in the investigation leading to the indictment.

With the return of a true bill by the grand jury in 1964, the FDA announced that seizure actions had already been started in Boston, Massachusetts, Washington, D. C., Baltimore, Maryland, Chicago, Illinois, Cincinnati, Ohio, Kansas City, Missouri, Providence, Rhode Island, and Lexington, Kentucky. This was the beginning of the end for Regimen Tablets.

The grand jury action marked the first time that defendants had ever been prosecuted under a combined indictment charging violations of laws enforced by the Post Office Department, the Department of Justice and the FDA. The indictment charged fraudulent use of television commercials, misbranding with intent to mislead, receiving money through the sale of Regimen Tablets by false and fraudulent means and conspiracy.

Some of the assertedly false statements used in newspaper and television advertising included these:

No-Diet Reducing With Regimen Tablets.

It's true! If you're normally healthy, you can lose as much as 70 pounds without cruel diet, without giving up all your favorite foods!

The only drug combination for your body to lose weight this fast-acting way.

The grand jury charged that endorsers of the product lost weight by other medication and/or by starvation diets; and that the defendants induced a doctor to change the conclusion of a clinical test he performed with Regimen from "fair to poor" to a favorable result, and that this fraudulent test was used in advertising.

In February, 1964, the charges against Arthur Herrick were dismissed after it was established that he was ill and a trial would endanger his life. Herrick was the president and sole stockholder of the New Drug Institute.

During the same month, the Criminal Court of the City of New York imposed fines upon the Drug Research Corporation, Andreadis and the advertising agency, after they pleaded guilty to charges of false and misleading advertising claims for Regimen within the state of New York.

At the trial of the Federal case in Brooklyn in 1965, the government showed that many persons who gave testimonials for magazine and television advertising of Regimen were actually reducing on starvation diets and drugs prescribed by physicians.

One New York woman said that she made $18,000 in nine months by appearing on "before and after" filmed commercials, ostensibly showing how she lost weight by taking Regimen Tablets. She said she was given a contract for appearances, and was paid fifty dollars extra for each pound she lost over fifteen pounds. She told the court that she did take Regimen—but she also went on a starvation diet while she was being weighed on "live" television shows.

Another woman who lost eighteen pounds in twenty-eight days, and an additional seven pounds in six weeks, had the same kind of deal—fifty dollars per pound for every pound lost over fifteen. She testified that during the six-week time span, she consumed less than five hundred calories a day, and during the last few days took nothing but black coffee, Diuril (to increase the system's liquid output) and phenobarbital, a sedative.

One man, who said he was instructed by the advertising agency to drink two quarts of water before the first weigh-in, lost twenty-eight pounds in twenty-eight days. Dr. Jean Mayer of Harvard University, a world-famous nutritional expert testifying for the government, said that this witness couldn't possibly have lost that much weight in such a short time, even if he'd eaten no food at all. The man then admitted that, in addition to Regimen, he also took thyroid pills.

The defendants elected not to call any witnesses in their behalf. The jury found John Andreadis, the Drug Research Corporation and the advertising agency guilty on several counts, including one food-and-drug charge. A subsequent motion for a mistrial was denied, and on June 25, 1965,

Federal Judge John R. Bartels fined the Drug Research Corporation $53,000, the advertising agency $50,000, and sentenced John Andreadis to eighteen months' imprisonment and to pay a fine of $50,000. Later, the New Drug Institute was fined $15,000.

It's estimated that the promoters of Regimen took ten million dollars from the weight-conscious public before they were stopped by injunctions and prosecution.

FDA's protection of the public against nutritional quackery is serious enough, but even more important is the agency's protective work in the field of drugs, many of which are of greater danger to health than foods for special dietary use.

5

Drug Dangers

ONE spring day the FDA received reports from a San Francisco hospital about startling reactions among children who were being given a standard drug treatment for tuberculosis. Little boys were developing oversized breasts and showing other signs of becoming like growing girls. The drug given the children was isonicotinic acid hydrazide tablets, long used effectively and without serious reactions in tuberculosis patients.

FDA inspectors hurried to the hospital and collected samples of the tablets. Analysis by chemists in the FDA's San Francisco laboratories showed that the pills were contaminated with stilbestrol, a potent female hormone.

The hospital stopped giving the drug, and the children soon returned to normal. But where and how did stilbestrol get into the TB drug, which was manufactured in New York, some three thousand miles away?

In New York, FDA men inspected the laboratory where the TB drug was made. They discovered that the firm used the same equipment to manufacture a number of drugs, and that the atmosphere in the plant was very dusty—an ideal situation for the cross-contamination of one drug with another. Analysis of various drug samples collected in the plant revealed small quantities of contaminants, including hormones, botanicals, insecticides and penicillin. In fact, of forty-nine samples collected in one month, eleven were found to be contaminated with differing amounts of penicillin.

Penicillin is light and fluffy, and is easily carried by air currents. The FDA survey showed that poor control of dust and poor cleaning of equipment used for both penicillin and other drugs were the two most important factors in drug contamination. The company, under FDA auspices, recalled the contaminated drugs from the market and took steps to prevent any recurrence.

This incident marked the beginning of a rash of similar troubles. A batch of penicillin sent by a large manufacturer for FDA certification was found to be contaminated with Tylosin, a veterinary drug. The company was at a loss to explain, because it produced Tylosin in one city and the penicillin in another. FDA inspectors discovered that the firm used sodium citrate as a buffering agent in both plants. A scoop had been used for both the Tylosin and the sodium citrate, so particles of the Tylosin had mixed with the citrate. The contaminated citrate had been shipped to the plant in the other city for use with the penicillin.

In still another drug company, the FDA found that an artificial sweetener was contaminated with penicillin. Analyses of drugs from other firms showed various amounts of penicillin that shouldn't have been there. Four lots of these drugs were recalled from the market.

Penicillin, the first of the so-called miracle antibiotics, has saved countless lives since it was introduced about 1940. However, it is estimated that about ten million Americans are so sensitized to the drug that its use by them could cause severe reactions or even death. In other words, to a great many people, penicillin is potentially dangerous, and its unknown presence in other drugs could have serious consequences.

The trouble pot boiled over when an FDA inspection of one of the largest drug manufacturers in the country revealed widespread cross-contamination of many drugs with penicillin. The FDA immediately suspended the firm's antibiotic certification privileges. The company shut down operations and, under FDA auspices, set in motion a vast recall operation to get its contaminated products off the market. Before the situation was brought under control, the company, monitored by FDA, retrieved and destroyed millions of dollars' worth of drugs and began an extensive program to correct faulty manufacturing processes and to separate penicillin production from all other operations.

The FDA now began a large sampling survey of penicillin producers to determine the extent of the problem. Analyses of more than eighty samples from ten different firms showed that contamination was widespread, mostly as a direct result of poor manufacturing methods.

The FDA next assembled a committee of some of the nation's leading medical scientists to advise it on the medical significance of penicillin contamination of other drugs. The committee reported that allergic reactions to penicillin may range from mild to fatal, and that all degrees of adverse reactions should be considered potentially dangerous. However, said the committee, very small amounts of penicillin might be allowed in other drugs as "reasonably safe" for use by individuals sensitive to penicillin. For injectable drugs it recommended a tolerance of less than .05 of a unit of penicillin for each maximum single dose, and for oral drugs less than .5 of a unit for each maximum single dose.

Using these recommendations as a basic guide, the FDA amended its regulations to prohibit the marketing of drugs contaminated with more than these amounts of penicillin. The agency also requested the drug industry to recall any products already on the market, or held in reserve, with penicillin contamination in excess of the tolerances.

By August 1, 1965, the FDA had inspected some fifty companies processing penicillin products, and twenty-two of these recalled four hundred batches of drugs contaminated with penicillin above the announced quantities. During August the FDA monitored the destruction of one million dollars' worth of antibiotics and other drugs contaminated with penicillin. Since that time the drug industry has taken steps to improve manufacturing operations. Several firms segregated penicillin production on separate floors or in separate buildings. Some discontinued penicillin production entirely.

Keeping watch on the nation's drug supply is a major FDA health activity. Basic to the program is the necessity for making sure that the manufacture, processing, packaging and labeling of drugs are done under controls adequate to insure that these products are safe and effective under the conditions for their use; that the drugs have the identity, strength, quality and purity claimed for them, and that they are correctly labeled.

FDA drug inspections cover all of these aspects. Inspectors check the condition and layout of buildings, departments and equipment (including laboratory instruments and experimental animals), and get information about the education, technical training and experience of key production and control employees.

The inspectors observe storage areas and procedures, compare master formulas and batch records for accuracy and completeness of information, determine what analyses or tests are run and the methods used. They note how weighing, measuring and mixing are done, how containers are cleaned, sterilized and stored, and whether laboratory controls and analyses are adequate. They carefully check procedures used to prevent labeling errors and mix-ups.

They inspect printing operations of the firms they visit. If a company contracts with commercial printers, the FDA suggests that the printing firm be carefully inspected before contracts are signed. The inspectors inquire into the checks made of the printed matter on labels, inserts and cartons, determine who supervises finishing operations and whether proper care is taken to see that products, labels, inserts and quantities are correct.

They check warehousing and shipping practices, inspect returned goods to determine the products, quantities and reasons for return, and to prevent mix-ups with salable stocks. They examine any complaints and learn what action is taken concerning them. Patterns and methods of distribution are checked, along with distribution records.

During an inspection—and always at its conclusion—any objectionable conditions or practices noted are pointed out to responsible management. Suggestions and recommendations are made at that time. During these discussions, or at the beginning of an inspection, the inspector inquires into the history of the business, its legal status, annual volume, and the percentage of interstate business. He asks whether raw materials are received from out-of-state sources, whether the firm is registered with FDA and what other governmental agencies inspect the company.

Each of these inspection points has subdivisions, but those described will give a general idea of the work and care that goes into the FDA inspection of drug firms.

Because of the rapid increase in the number of new drugs after World War II, many physicians found it difficult to keep abreast of the field through routine medical communications. Providing information about new drugs became a major function of drug manufacturers, and very often doctors obtained most of their information about a new drug through the maker's advertising and promotion systems. But the doctors were not always told about a new drug's side effects, dangers or undesirability.

To remedy this situation, in 1961 the FDA issued a regulation requiring that a package insert be on or inside of all prescription-drug packages. This "full disclosure" regulation required that "labeling on or within the packages from which the drug is to be dispensed bears adequate information for its use, including indications, effects, dosages, routes, methods, and frequency and duration of administration, and any relevant hazards, contraindications, side effects and precautions under which practitioners licensed by law to administer the drug can use the drug safely and for the purposes for which it is intended, including all purposes for which it is advertised or represented. . . ."

The fact is that virtually all drugs can be harmful. In testimony before a Congressional committee, Dr. James L. Goddard, Commissioner of Food and Drugs, said, "Drugs are intended to affect physiological functioning of the body. Thus the values of the effect of a drug must be weighed against the dangers of the disease or condition being attacked. No drug can ever be guaranteed completely safe. You do not have 'safe drugs' on the one hand and 'unsafe drugs' on the other. When we talk about drug safety, we are talking about relative safety."

When a drug manufacturer begins research on the effects of a new drug he files an "investigational new drug" (IND) notice with the FDA. The investigation customarily involves experimental animals first, then human beings—provided the humans consent and are made fully aware of the drug's purposes and probable effects. At this stage the FDA can stop all human trials if animal experimentation is considered inadequate, if the investigational plan is not considered sound, if experience shows continued investigation to be unsafe, or for a number of other reasons. The proper testing of a new drug may take many months, or even years.

If and when a manufacturer finally applies for approval to market the new drug commercially, he submits a "new drug application" (NDA) which contains or refers to all evidence upon which he bases his belief that the product is safe and effective.

For example, an NDA must include:

Results of tests on animals.

Results of tests on humans.

Names and qualifications of the investigators who tested the drug.

A list of all ingredients, and amounts of each, in the formula.

A description of manufacturing procedures.

A description of tests and checks made to assure purity, strength and reliability, and to prevent errors in manufacture.

Qualifications of personnel who supervised the drug's manufacture.

All proposed labels and accompanying literature.

Under the law, when a package insert indicates that a certain drug is for a specific purpose, it must be proved that the drug is safe and effective for that purpose. The proof must be in the form of adequate, well-controlled studies conducted by scientists or doctors who have the training and experience to interpret such studies. This information is usually submitted to the FDA in a form similar to that of an article in a medical journal. The doctor outlines his objectives, his selection of patients, safety and efficacy tests and the various aspects to be measured. Unlike a journal article, however, the report also includes the patients' work sheets. From these it is possible to reconstruct a study and draw an independent and perhaps different interpretation. As a rule, studies by more than one well-qualified investigator are required to substantiate the efficacy of a drug for a particular indication. The information in a "new drug application" may total many volumes of facts, figures, slides, charts and other scientific data.

Information about adverse reactions reaches the FDA through several channels, the most important being the drug manufacturers themselves. The manufacturers are required by FDA regulations to file quarterly reports on the drug for the first year it is marketed, semiannual reports the second year, and annual reports thereafter. These contain all adverse experiences the company knows about, summaries of additional animal and clinical trials and any new information relating to the safety and efficacy of the drug.

Additional information comes from the FDA Hospital Reporting System, a network of some eighty-five hospitals across the country under contract to report on the adverse effects of drugs. Also, doctors and patients often report reactions and adverse effects directly to the FDA, and regular biyearly inspections of manufacturing plants and records occasionally turn up adverse reaction reports which have not reached the FDA for one reason or another.

To keep up with the growing mass of information about investigational and new drugs, the FDA has an electronic computer which can swiftly provide names and addresses of clinical investigators, adverse reactions caused by various drugs, histories of patients, diagnoses and treatments, data from FDA research programs evaluating animal reactions to different compounds, histories of food samples examined for pesticide residues—and a lot of other helpful information.

More than 90 percent of the drugs called for in prescriptions today have been developed since 1938, when the Food, Drug and Cosmetic Act of 1938 required, for the first time, that a new drug be proved safe before it is marketed.

The Kefauver-Harris Amendments of 1962 extended this requirement to provide that there must also be substantial evidence that a drug will be effective for its intended purpose. New drugs, previously cleared, may be removed from the market if new information indicates they are hazardous to health or ineffective for their intended use.

Each NDA is evaluated by FDA scientists—medical officers, pharmacologists, chemists—who must decide whether the usefulness of the drug outweighs its possible dangers. All experimental data, both animal and human, are reviewed. A single NDA may consist of up to eighty volumes of data, requiring months to evaluate. Many applications present novel medical problems and new therapeutic approaches to treatment of diseases. In such cases, advisory committees or individual experts are consulted to reach the soundest decision possible in the light of current medical knowledge.

If the drug is approved, but is one that can be used safely and effectively only by or under the supervision of a physician, it will be released for sale only by prescription. Labeling information for such drugs is intended for the physicians who will prescribe them.

Once the drug is approved, no changes may be made in its active ingredients, although inactive (harmless) components may be changed. If any active ingredient is changed or added or deleted, the drug again becomes a new drug and subject to FDA approval. Aspirin tablets usually contain not more than five grains of aspirin. If a barbiturate were added to aspirin, the "new drug" procedure would apply. Also, if the label on a container of aspirin recommended larger dosages than those already approved, the aspirin might be considered a new drug until the increased dosage was found to be "safe and effective."

One of the most-publicized actions in FDA history concerned a drug with the generic name "thalidomide" that was first marketed in West Germany in 1957. By 1960 its sales had skyrocketed, and through licensing arrangements between the manufacturer and foreign drug companies, thalidomide was available in Great Britain, Canada, Portugal and other countries, but not in the United States. Used as a sleeping tablet, sedative and antiemetic (to stop vomiting) in pregnancy, the drug became renowned for a desirable safety feature: unlike most other sedatives, it would not cause death, even when taken in large doses.

In September, 1960, after nearly two years of animal and clinical testing, an American drug company submitted a new drug application to the FDA to market thalidomide under the trade name Kevadon. The company was so confident of quick FDA approval that it assembled key salesmen to line up hospital doctors for a final round of clinical trials, simply to "confirm" thalidomide's usefulness. But the salesmen were told that the main purpose was to establish local studies whose results could be spread among hospital staff members. Doctors were assured that they need not report results if they chose not to. In all, more than twelve hundred investigators (doctors) were given free samples, and nearly twenty thousand patients were treated.

In the FDA's Division of New Drugs, Dr. Frances O. Kelsey, a forty-eight-year-old woman physician, was given the drug to process. Dr. Kelsey believed that the evidence submitted by the drug company did not show beyond question that the drug was safe. By pressure of letters, telephone calls and personal visits, the company tried to hasten FDA approval, but Dr. Kelsey held firm and asked for additional data.

One day she read a doctor's letter to the editor of the *British Medical Journal*. The writer wondered if thalidomide might be responsible for four cases he had observed of peripheral neuritis, a deterioration of the nerves in the hands and feet. A similar discovery in West Germany led authorities to change the drug's status from over-the-counter to prescription sales. Dr. Kelsey considered that if thalidomide did produce such an ailment it might be hazardous to an unborn child whose pregnant mother took the drug.

While the American drug company was briefing its salesmen, two cases of phocomelia were described by a German doctor to a pediatric convention. Phocomelia is a congenital deformity in which hands or feet are attached to the human trunk by single, very short bones—like flippers on a seal. The word itself is derived from two Greek words meaning "seal" and "limb."

Reports began to come in of German babies born by the hundreds with this terrible malformation. A German physician suspected the cause to be thalidomide tablets taken by mothers during the first three months of pregnancy. Hearing of this widespread affliction, another American woman physician, Dr. Helen B. Taussig of the Johns Hopkins University Pediatrics Department, went to Germany to get firsthand information. She came home to spread the word by letters, public lectures and in print about thalidomide's horrifying effects. Dr. Kelsey went to Baltimore to talk with Dr. Taussig.

On March 8, 1962, the American drug company asked Dr.

Kelsey that its new-drug application for thalidomide be withdrawn.

Had Dr. Kelsey been less unyielding, and had Kevadon been released, some ten thousand deformed babies might have been born in the United States before the reason was known. That a smaller scale disaster didn't take place was remarkable, considering the wide distribution of Kevadon by the drug company to clinical investigators. Much of the record-keeping by these doctors was nonexistent or shoddy, and the FDA had a hard time making sure that all supplies of the drug were recalled or destroyed. As it was, only a few cases of phocomelia occurred in America, mostly from thalidomide obtained abroad.

Dr. Kelsey was presented with the Gold Medal Award for Distinguished Civilian Service by President John F. Kennedy.

The FDA laws and regulations regarding new drugs do not apply to the experimental use of narcotics, which are subject to regulation by the Federal Bureau of Narcotics, U. S. Treasury Department, Washington, D. C. 20220. This bureau is to be transferred to the Department of Justice.

Biologic drugs, made from living organisms and their products (rabies vaccine, dog distemper vaccines, etc.) for use in lower animals are subject to licensing provisions enforced by the Veterinary Biologics Division, U. S. Department of Agriculture, Hyattsville, Maryland 20782.

Biologic drugs (vaccines, serums, antitoxins) for use in humans are controlled by licensing provisions enforced by the Division of Biologics Standards, U. S. Public Health Service, Bethesda, Maryland 20014.

Several hundred "new drug applications" are received yearly for medicated feeds and veterinary drugs. The prevention, control or treatment of livestock diseases is a highly important aspect of modern agriculture; the use of small quantities of potent drugs in balanced animal feeds can help to keep stock healthy and increase growth. However, medicated feeds must be produced and used within the limits of safety to avoid animal injury and residues in food for humans. Thus the FDA carefully reviews each application to see that drug manufacturers use proper care in preparing, testing and mixing the products, and that feed mills have suitable facilities to produce safe and effective feeds.

Veterinarians and pharmacologists of the FDA's Bureau of Medicine maintain a "farm" for basic research on animal health and pathology in Beltsville, Maryland, where they check drugs, devices and claims made by manufacturers. These studies may vary from investigations of the potassium requirements of sheep to an evaluation of a contact lens for chickens. It's true—a manufacturer produced contact lenses for chickens, with the claim that this prevented cannibalism and pecking each other within the flock. The FDA test chickens were fitted with the lenses, which they quickly scratched out. After learning of these test results, the manufacturer promptly removed his product from the market.

Treatments for pinkeye in animals and commercial tonics for chickens were also tested. Neither preparation was effective. The FDA veterinarians also test products intended for human use. For instance, a pig's skin is similar to human skin in many ways, so pigs and monkeys were used to test a cosmetic for which unusual claims had been made. No significant changes were observed during the test period.

The FDA keeps constant vigilance to assure that our milk supply is free from harmful quantities of residues of drugs, antibiotics and pesticides. In one continuing project, five chlorinated pesticides were fed to cows at varying levels, and the milk was tested for residues. In another, four antibiotics were given to cows, and when three were found to leave abnormal residues, the products were not permitted to be marketed.

Seizures have been made of medicated feeds that contained drugs stronger or weaker than the declared potency. Some feeds are seized because of drug contamination or because they fail to contain drugs alleged to be in them. Many of the applications for medicated feeds or veterinary drugs are not approved because manufacturers' tests are considered incomplete and inadequate to prove the safety and effectiveness of the drugs, or because the FDA scientists have established that the drugs are unsafe.

A program for veterinary medicine, similar to the adverse reaction reporting system in human medicine, was started by the FDA in 1965. Under this plan, veterinary medical colleges and clinics report to the FDA the adverse reactions and other helpful observations relating to drug safety and efficacy encountered in their studies. Similar programs are also planned for veterinarians who practice in large clinics or animal hospitals.

In some years the FDA has turned down three to five times as many drug applications as it has approved. A few of the reasons: 45 percent didn't have enough animal safety data; 72 percent failed to show adequate clinical safety to permit commercial marketing; 76 percent lacked facts to show clinical efficacy; in 41 percent, component and composition data were inadequate. In 71 percent the applications did not describe manufacturing controls which the FDA felt would assure a quality drug product. Samples submitted were unacceptable in 46 percent of those returned, and in 53 percent of the rejected applications the FDA refused to allow the proposed labeling.

The yearly average of NDA's received (for human use) is about 180, of which about sixty-eight are approved.

In 1965 the FDA found that 14 percent (about 4,600) of all drug samples it collected were in violation of regulations, and 21 percent (about 3,200) of establishments inspected revealed violations. In prescription drugs alone, 32 percent were violative. There were 322 FDA seizure actions involving such practices and deficiencies as:

No approved "new drug application."

Inadequate directions for use.

False and misleading claims.

Low potency.

Noncompliance with U. S. Pharmacopeia standards.

Imitations.

Below purported quality.

The number of shortcomings and deficiencies in production, processing and marketing of drugs was also shown by more than three hundred separate instances in which drugs had to be recalled from the market. Both large and small firms were involved, and many of the recalls represented major hazards to health, such as:

Label mix-ups.

Penicillin cross-contamination.

Two different drugs in one bottle.

Low potency.

Excess potency.

Ingredient substitution.

NDA withdrawal ⎫
IND termination ⎭ because of hazards to health.

In the face of these findings the FDA said, "The number of serious violations demonstrates that insufficient protection is being given the American consumer in this critical area of dangerous discrepancies."

Another critical area of vital importance to the FDA and the public lies in a different aspect of the drug field. It concerns barbiturates and amphetamines—the latter popularly known as "pep pills" or "bennies," and widely used by truck drivers and others to ward off sleep.

Although enforcement activities in this field were to be transferred to the Department of Justice in 1968, the pioneering work of FDA's Bureau of Drug Abuse Control is deserving of recognition and is included as an important part of the FDA story.

6

Bennies, Barbs, and Beedack

ONE afternoon on the Iowa Turnpike an Air-Force sergeant, his wife, two small children and the family dog were stopped by highway officials making a routine traffic survey. More than half a mile to the rear were signs with slow-down warnings. The signs were ignored by the driver of a huge tractor-trailer that came barreling down the road with no letup in speed. Before the family or the highway officials realized what was happening, the roaring giant slammed into the sergeant's car and crumpled it like a cardboard box. The car burst into flames. Every member of the family was mangled and burned beyond recognition.

The driver of the truck was not seriously hurt, but he seemed dazed—and no wonder. Investigators found that he had driven 980 miles in thirty straight hours, taking pep pills to stay awake. Three bottles of the pills were found in his luggage.

In West Virginia, a tractor flatbed truck swerved suddenly to the wrong side of the turnpike and crashed into an oncoming mobile post office. Both drivers were killed, along with three postal employees sorting mail inside the post-office vehicle. Officers found pep pills in the tractor flatbed cab, and an analysis of the contents of the tractor driver's stomach showed that he had taken some of the tablets.

The amphetamines, which include pep pills, directly stimulate the central nervous system. They produce alertness (up to a point), excitation, increased activity and an ability to go without sleep for lengthy periods. In legitimate medical usage, amphetamines are prescribed to reduce the appetites of overweight patients, or in cases of narcolepsy (a disorder that creates a great desire for sleep), or for Parkinson's disease (a form of paralysis), or for certain kinds of minor mental depression.

Persons who abuse the drug increase their doses gradually, because the body builds up a tolerance to amphetamines. The increased dosages wildly exaggerate the normal effects and result in excitability, talkativeness, tremors of the hands, enlarged pupils of the eyes and heavy perspiration. In serious cases a psychosis resembling schizophrenia develops, with delusions and hallucinations. These effects are particularly dangerous to long-distance drivers. They take amphetamines to ward off sleep, and may be completely unaware of how tired they really are until their fatigue overcomes them and causes serious highway accidents. Sometimes the desired effect may wear off while a truck or car is traveling at high speed. The driver falls asleep, perhaps never to wake again.

Criminals frequently use amphetamines to increase their courage and alertness during the commission of crimes.

Although amphetamines do not cause physical addiction, abusers do develop psychic or emotional dependence upon these drugs, and continued abuse of them can cause high blood pressure, abnormal heart rhythms and even heart attacks.

Amphetamines are known to drug abusers as "pep pills," "wake-ups," "eye-openers," "copilots," "truck drivers," or "bennies." As with other dangerous drugs, slang names are also frequently based upon the shapes and colors of capsules and tablets, their effects, or their uses. Some examples:

1. Amphetamine sulfate in rose-colored heart-shaped tablet is known as "peaches," "roses," "hearts" or "bennies."
2. Amphetamine sulfate in round, white, double-scored tablets is called "cartwheels," "whites" or "bennies."
3. Long-acting amphetamine sulfate capsules, found in many colors, are known as "coast-to-coasts," "LA turnabouts," "co-pilots" or "browns."
4. Amphetamine sulfate oval-shaped tablets of various colors are called "footballs" or "greenies."
5. Amphetamine for injection, in abuser jargon, is called "speed," "bombido," "jugs" or "bottles."
6. Dextroamphetamine sulfate in orange-colored heart-shaped tablets is known as "hearts," "oranges" or "dexies."

Opposite to the amphetamines are depressants, including the barbiturates. Barbiturates *depress* the central nervous system, and doctors sometimes prescribe them in small doses to induce sleep. They are also valuable in cases of acute anxiety, hyperthyroidism and high blood pressure. Because of their sedative effects, barbiturates are used in treating both physical and mental illnesses.

Continued and excessive doses of barbiturates, however, result in the slurring of speech, staggering, loss of balance, falling, quick temper and quarrelsome dispositions. An overdose, particularly when taken in conjunction with alcohol, will probably result in unconsciousness and death unless the victim gets proper medical treatment in time.

Physical dependence upon barbiturates doesn't usually develop with dosages normally prescribed for medical reasons, but it does occur with the excessive amounts used by drug abusers. A tolerance is also developed—and the symptoms of withdrawal are generally far more dangerous than those resulting from a withdrawal of narcotics such as heroin.

Barbiturates are known to drug abusers as "barbs," "candy," "goofballs," "sleeping pills" or "peanuts." As with the amphetamines, specific types are often named after their color or shape. For instance:

1. Pentobarbital sodium, in solid yellow capsule form, is known as "yellows," "yellow jackets" or "nimbles" (after a trade name of this drug).
2. Secobarbital sodium in red capsule form is called "reds," "pinks," "redbirds," "red devils" and "seggy" or "secky" (after trade names).
3. Amobarbital sodium combined with secobarbital sodium, in red and blue capsules, is known as "rainbows," "red-and-blues" or "double trouble."
4. Amobarbital sodium, in solid blue capsule form, is known by abusers as "blues," "bluebirds," "blue devils" or "blue heavens."

According to the FDA, "Trafficking in dangerous drugs—particularly amphetamines—continues to increase in volume and scope despite efforts directed to the activities of large operators. The business is moving out of the hands of small amateur peddlers into the realm of large wholesale distributors who are aware of enforcement activities and go to unusual lengths to avoid arrest. Many are members of organized rackets."

Problems relating to another dangerous drug—the hallucinogen called LSD—are discussed in Chapter 7.

Until 1966 the FDA inspectors were responsible for the enforcement work done by the FDA in the field of illegal dangerous drugs. They also had to perform their regular inspection duties, they had no powers of arrest and they could not carry firearms. They depended heavily upon the cooperation of the Bureau of Narcotics and state and local police.

Because of increasing national concern over the spreading abuse of hallucinogens, depressants and stimulants, Congress in 1965 enacted certain Drug Abuse Control Amendments to the Food, Drug and Cosmetic Act, and the amendments became effective on February 1, 1966. As a newly authorized enforcement arm, the FDA set up a Bureau of Drug Abuse Control (BDAC) with headquarters in Washington, and a number of field offices from Boston to Los Angeles.

To carry out the new provisions of the law, more than three hundred specially trained BDAC agents are empowered to seize illegal supplies of the controlled drugs, to serve warrants and to arrest persons engaged in the illegal manufacture, trade or handling of dangerous drugs. The agents have the right to carry firearms while engaged in the performance of their duties.

The law now has a double-barreled approach to curb drug abuse. All legal handlers of dangerous drugs must keep records of their supplies and sales. Those who produce, sell or distribute drugs illegally are liable to arrest, prosecution and imprisonment. Because of the serious consequences of drug abuse among young people, special penalties are provided for persons over eighteen years old who sell or give any controlled drugs to those under twenty-one. The first offense carries a maximum penalty of two years in prison, or a fine of not more than $5,000, or both. The second offense calls for a maximum of six years in prison or a fine of not more than $15,000, or both.

The drug abuser finds various ways to get dangerous drugs unlawfully. He may alter the date and dosage of an existing prescription, or forge a new one on a prescription pad stolen from a doctor's office. He may purchase pep pills or barbiturates from peddlers at truck stops, newsstands, bars or other hangouts. He may even have a working arrangement with an unscrupulous pharmacist.

Dangerous drugs get into the illicit retail trade through thefts from reputable manufacturers, wholesalers or drug stores. Bootleg manufacturers operate unlawfully in garages, basements and warehouses to produce substantial quantities. Counterfeiters make dangerous drugs, and some registered manufacturers also dispose of such drugs through the illicit trade. The bulk peddler is an important link in the traffic—he deals in hundreds of thousands of capsules and tablets of dangerous drugs. Billions of capsules and pills are produced every year in the United States, and more than a few billion find their way into the hands of drug abusers by way of the black market.

Since January, 1967, the FDA has offered state and local law-enforcement agencies a free laboratory service for chemical and microbiological analysis of any drug submitted in accordance with instructions available from the BDAC. The service is performed by experts in FDA's Bureau of Science.

Most tablets can be identified by "pillistics," a method developed by the FDA. The term is derived from "ballistics," in which it is recognized that a gun will produce distinctive markings on bullets fired from it, so that a bullet can identify the gun from which it was shot.

In "pillistics" a machine punch will produce characteristic markings on tablets stamped by it; therefore, a tablet can identify the punch and the manufacturer of the pill. This method is used to prove interstate commerce in illicit sales of drugs, and also to detect counterfeit drugs. Fewer counterfeit drugs are encountered today, perhaps as the result of early FDA successes in discouraging bootleg manufacturers. Most of the counterfeits are imitations of amphetamines and barbiturates, which have a ready sale among eager drug abusers.

When Winton B. Rankin, Assistant FDA Commissioner, testified before a Congressional committee on appropriations, the subject of counterfeit drugs was discussed. Congressman Daniel J. Flood of Pennsylvania asked how counterfeiters could market their products. "Here's a drug store or a physician," Mr. Flood said. "Is it just corruption and bribery? Why would a druggist who knows and buys from B, C and D companies, and knows the drug, buy from Joe Zilch?"

Mr. Rankin answered, "We broke up a counterfeiting ring a few years ago, operated by a man and his son. They put counterfeit drugs in packages that looked like the genuine articles, then traveled from one drug store to another and told purchasers that through special buying arrangements they had been able to get a special price, so they offered the drugs at a special price."

MR. FLOOD. They were con men besides?

MR. RANKIN. They were con men. I'm not trying to excuse the druggists who bought. They ought to have sense enough to know you don't get good drugs at a very low price.

What kinds of people are the drug abusers? Although many of them have personality disorders, they come from all social and economic levels—wealthy, poor and in between. The adult abuser often finds that drugs lower a chemical curtain between him and reality. He feels inferior in a competitive world, and although outwardly he may seem successful in his occupation, he has deep feelings of insecurity. He dreads the decisions, the crises and the problems of each day. He may have come to drugs by way of alcohol, or during an illness when drugs were administered in treatment.

He discovers that continual pill taking is not frowned upon by society as are alcoholism and narcotic addiction. He takes drugs to go to sleep, to wake up, to be alert or to be comfortably calm, despite the fact that he also develops a psychic or a physical dependence upon the drugs.

Young people face a very different world. Adolescence, under the best of circumstances, is a time of difficulty and stress. The adolescent doesn't understand himself and often finds little real understanding at home, so he seeks refuge among groups or gangs of other young people who go through the same difficulties. This satisfies his need to be understood, to be accepted and to belong.

In order to gain recognition in his group, the young person must conform to its code of behavior. He defies legal, social and parental authority, and plays follow-the-leader in novel experiences, experiments and thrills. Experimentation often begins with sniffing airplane glue, lighter fluid, gasoline or ether. It may advance into the use of barbiturates or amphet-amines—which the leader of the group can usually produce at a minimum of cost. Acceptance by the group is no longer enough—the juvenile now seeks its approval, and he can best gain it by not turning away from the dangerous drugs used by his companions. Once he finds that potent drugs are easily available, he is well on the way to becoming a confirmed drug abuser.

How do the peddlers of pep pills work? How are they put out of business? I talked with officials of the BDAC (they call it "Beedack") who gave me details of a fairly typical case.

In November, 1966, G. J. (Jack) Bologna, then BDAC agent in charge of the Baltimore District, received a telephone call from his counterpart in New York City.

"We've just nabbed a trucker for selling twenty thousand bennies to other drivers," the New York agent said. "In his pocket we found a paper with a North Carolina phone number and the name 'Jim.' We figure Jim must be his contact, but our guy won't talk."

The Baltimore District had jurisdiction in North Carolina, and one of Bologna's agents was a native of that state. Bologna had him call the number. A woman answered.

"Is Jim there?" the agent asked.

"No, he ain't. He's outa town. What you want him for?"

105

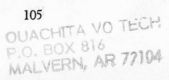

"When'll he be back?"

"Couple days. Wanta leave a message?"

"No. I'll call later."

"Was it about pills?" the woman asked.

"I'll call in a couple of days."

"Who is this? What's your name?'

"Ralph. But he don't know me. Just tell him Ralph will call him."

Two days later Ralph called again and reached Jim.

"I want to get some pills," Ralph said.

"How come you're callin' me?"

"What difference? Word gets around. I need some bennies to peddle in West Virginia. You want to sell me some or not?"

"Well," Jim said, "if you want to come down here, we can talk about it better than over the phone."

A check with the North Carolina State Bureau of Investigation showed that Jim was a truck driver who hauled produce. Pep pills were his sideline. Agents of the state bureau were assigned to cooperate with the BDAC men.

Ralph and another agent flew to North Carolina and, as previously agreed, met Jim at the airport. They sat in the suspect's car and talked.

"How many pills you-all want?" Jim asked.

"Depends on your price," Ralph said. "How much?"

"Depends on how many. How many?"

"Ten thousand."

"Seven hundred bucks."

Ralph scowled. "What! Seven hundred? Man, you're outa your mind!"

"That's the goin' price hereabouts," Jim said.

"Yeah? Well, if you can't do better'n that, you can keep

'em. No deal." Ralph and his companion started to leave the car.

"Wait, now, hold on there," Jim said, grabbing Ralph's arm. "What'd you expect to pay?"

"Five hundred—tops. If we shopped around, we could prob'ly get 'em for less, but we don't have time. Five hundred —take it or leave it."

Jim looked thoughtful, then nodded. "Okay, it's a deal. When do you want delivery?"

"Right now."

"Oh, no. Oh, no. I don't carry the stuff around. I gotta go get 'em."

"How do I know your stuff is good?"

"I guarantee it. Besides, you ain't heard squawks from any of my other customers, have you?"

"No—but I don't trust anybody. I want a sample. You got a sample with you?"

Jim reached into a coat pocket and brought out a small bottle containing some white tablets. He took one out and handed it to the agent. Ralph said, "I'm going to the men's room. Be right back."

In the men's room Ralph made a quick test of the pill. Not only the BDAC agents, but also most underworld buyers of pep pills have kits with which they can make tests to be sure the pills are amphetamines and not merely worthless or caffeine tablets. Caffeine also wards off sleep for some people.

The sample proved to be amphetamine. The agent paid Jim $250 in cash, with the understanding that Jim would get the pills and pick up the balance of $250 upon delivery. When he left the airport, Jim was followed by agents who had kept the car under surveillance and who hoped to identify his source of supply, but they lost him in heavy traffic. In a little while he returned to the airport, delivered the pills and received the remaining $250. He wasn't arrested, because the agents hoped to make a later deal and find his source.

Back in Baltimore the pills were analyzed. There were some seven different kinds, and some were not genuine amphetamines.

In a few days Ralph tried to telephone Jim for another delivery but couldn't reach him. On Christmas Eve in Baltimore, the agent tried again. This time he talked with Jim, who was receptive.

"I'm hauling a load of vegetables to New York tonight," Jim said. "I could meet you near Annapolis. You want the same deal?"

"Same deal."

There was one difficulty. Ralph didn't have $500 in cash, and official funds wouldn't be available until banks opened the day after Christmas. The agent in charge, Jack Bologna, explained the situation to his other agents. They all pooled enough of their personal cash to make the $500 payment.

Ralph met Jim near Annapolis, as agreed, and made the buy. Once again Jim wasn't picked up, but the agents now went to the United States attorney in Baltimore and obtained an arrest warrant for Jim. A couple of days later, Ralph telephoned him to place another pill order.

"I won't be home for a couple of days," Jim said, "but if you're in a hurry you can get the stuff from my wife at the house."

The next morning Ralph and other BDAC men joined

agents of the North Carolina Bureau of Investigation and went to the vicinity of Jim's home. Ralph approached the house alone as the others watched from a distance.

Jim's wife handed Ralph a package of five thousand pep pills.

"That's not enough," Ralph said. "The weather's cold, and the drivers are asking for more stuff. Don't you have any more here?"

"No, not here. But I can get some more from my girl friend Betty."

Jim's wife called Betty, asking her to deliver ten thousand pills. The wife also vouched for the reliability of her "customer."

"I'll come over and put the pills on your porch," Betty said. "You collect the money and pay us later."

Within a few minutes Betty arrived and put a package on the porch. As she started to leave, she was arrested by the agents. Jim's wife was also taken into custody. When asked where she obtained her pills, Betty said she got them from her husband and that they had more at home. With her consent the agents searched her house and seized 96,000 tablets.

"Who's the supplier?" they asked. "Who makes this stuff?"

The girl told them that the pills came from a man named Charlie Smith in a nearby Virginia town. Smith was known to BDAC agents as having a previous criminal record for peddling drugs.

The agents now sought cooperation from the Virginia State Police and tried to obtain a search warrant for Smith's home. A Federal judge refused to issue the warrant until a stronger "probable cause" was established. However, the Virginia State Police did get a search warrant from a Justice of the

Peace, and four state troopers and two BDAC agents went to Smith's place.

In the house they arrested Smith and his wife, along with Betty's husband. In an outbuilding near the house they seized 75,000 pep pills. Smith carried $23,000 in his pockets. His wife had $5,000.

Smith insisted that the pills represented his entire stock, and he was anxious to leave with the officers. As one agent said later, "He was too eager to go. That made us suspicious."

The BDAC agents returned to the basement of the house and began to rap on the walls. One had a hollow sound, and the agents discovered that the wall was actually a thin partition and that it concealed a substantial batch of bennies—more than 325 million tablets!

This haul represented a fortune in black-market money (about $32.5 million) since the tablets could sell (at retail) for ten cents each or more at that time. As of 1968 the retail price has gone up, partly because the BDAC agents were making it tough for dealers to operate. The price at the beginning of 1968 was thirty-five cents per "set," or three sets for a dollar. A set is one amphetamine and one barbiturate— "one up, one down."

Names used for the foregoing account are fictitious, but the facts are as told to me by Agent Bologna. He also said that Smith's wife pleaded guilty, was fined $1,000 and placed on probation for two years. Smith was convicted, fined $1,000 and sentenced to one year in prison and five years probation. Jim and his wife were also fined and placed on probation.

Some cases don't require extensive investigation. In Oklahoma, for instance, a "sanitarium" operator (unlicensed) was known to sell prescription drugs. FDA inspectors, posing as customers, were readily ushered into his "examination room," which was lined with shelves holding drugs. "It was like shopping in a supermarket," the inspectors said later. "We just walked around and picked up whatever drugs we wanted to buy!"

The operator was arrested, and the FDA seized $40,000 worth of prescription drugs. The man had a long history of convictions for violating Federal and state laws.

In a single year the FDA initiated more than 150 drug prosecution cases against 232 firms and individuals charged with unlawful sale of prescription drugs. Drug stores or pharmacists, or both, were involved in sixty-four of the cases. Two doctors were prosecuted for selling amphetamines, barbiturates and other prescription drugs to persons for nonmedical purposes. Many cases involved peddlers at truck-stops and drive-in restaurants.

To the BDAC, it is as important to fight abuse of barbiturates as abuse of amphetamines. One of their most unusual cases was in the area of Newport and Covington, Kentucky. For five years the FDA district office had received complaints that barbiturates and knockout drops were being sold in both places, and that teenagers and criminals could buy the drugs without difficulty. Many sales were made through local bars.

FDA investigators established that the sales were engineered by one man who employed subdistributors to peddle the drugs on street corners and in taverns. Each peddler worked in a restricted "territory" and would be discharged if he invaded another's zone. An undercover BDAC agent succeeded in buying five thousand barbiturates and 25,000 pep pills from the top man, who was arrested when he made delivery. He and nine of his peddlers were sent to jail.

A self-styled "doctor" running a "clinic" in a western state sold large quantities of barbiturates and antibiotics to undercover FDA inspectors. He was arrested, sent to jail for two years and fined $1,000. State authorities issued an injunction prohibiting him from practicing medicine.

Two reputable physicians in Indiana and Kentucky were selling barbiturates and amphetamines to practically anybody —including FDA investigators who posed as truck and taxi drivers.

In Juneau, Alaska, a drug store was fined $1,000 and one man $500 for dispensing barbiturates, tranquilizers and amphetamines without prescriptions.

A Pittsburgh, Pennsylvania, teenage boy found drugged led to the discovery of his drug source, a pharmacy. The store was known to supply barbiturates and pep pills to other teenagers. Local police and FDA inspectors were able to buy drugs without prescriptions. The two store operators were arrested and fined $1,000.

An unusual case in Minneapolis, Minnesota, involved the sale of barbiturates and amphetamines to high-school students by a man who distributed the drugs from a wheelchair in his home.

Many doctors rightfully claim that they have prescribed barbiturates for years without changing patients into addicts. In some cases, however, evidence shows that barbiturates prescribed by doctors are decidedly harmful. Movie actress Marilyn Monroe took barbiturates, sedatives and tranquilizers in large doses, and killed herself. Just before her suicide she refilled a prescription for fifty pentobarbital capsules, even

FDA's laboratory building in Washington, D.C. is the largest and most modern facility in the world devoted to research on foods, drugs and cosmetics.

FDA Photo

James L. Goddard, Commissioner the Food & Drug Administration, W.

Dr. Harvey W. Wiley headed the first Federal food and drug agency in 1907. He has been called "Father of the Food and Drug Act."

FDA Photo

FDA Photo

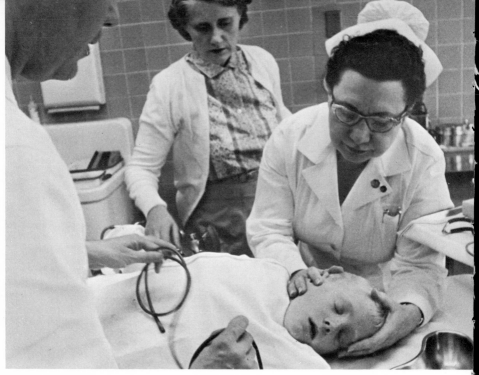

Accidental poisoning from hazardous household substances accounted for 40% of fatal poisonings in one year, of children under five. Doctors reported over 90,000 cases like this emergency room scene.   *FDA Photo*

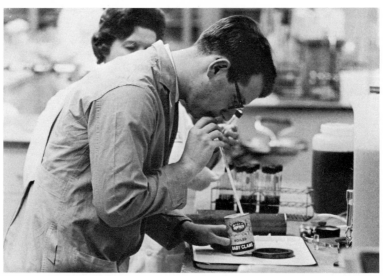

FDA laboratory technician uses pipette to obtain sample of clam broth for bacterial analysis.   *FDA Photo*

First step in ashing of food sample for radioactivity analysis.
Sample is burned over electric stove in FDA lab, then baked in
oven at right.

FDA Photo

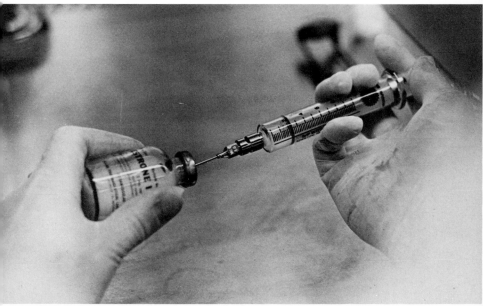

n sterile environment, drug sample is drawn to be planted in
culture to learn whether any bacteria is present.

FDA Photo

Consumer protection is FDA's main goal. This child can be sure the food she is about to eat is pure, wholesome and clean.

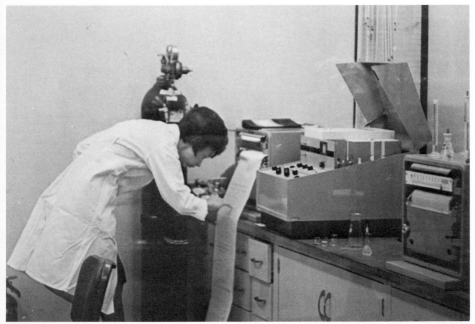

An FDA chemist studies readings from a gas chromatograph. This machine analyzes food samples to detect pesticide residues.

FDA scientists check potency of all antibiotics made in the United States or imported.

An FDA scientist checks a New Drug Application (NDA) for technical data. Information on a single NDA may fill dozens of folders.

An FDA chemist filtering a drug sample. She has reduced a pill to its compounds and will now measure the filtered product for potency and strength.

Capsule inspectors check for imperfections in filled capsules at A. H. Robins Company, Richmond (Va.) pharmaceutical manufacturer. Each lot of capsules is inspected at least twice before being packaged.

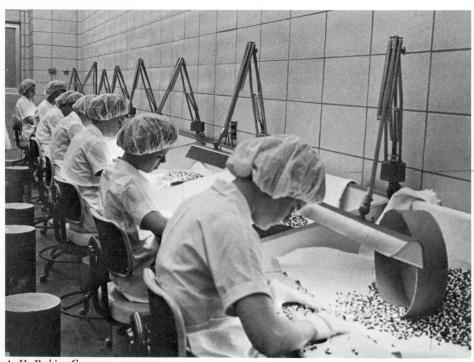

Judy Hughes of E. R. Squibb & Sons checks one of nearly 1200 volumes of research material sent to the FDA by Squibb to support medical effectiveness of 96 Squibb drugs cleared for safety by the FDA between 1938 and 1962. Data is for review by experts selected by National Academy of Sciences National Research Council.

Squibb Division

In FDA's Data Control Center an IBM computer helps to study new drugs not yet released for marketing.

FDA Photo

FDA inspector checks label information on ingredient used in pill-coating process of drug manufacturer. *FDA Photo*

Experts at Parke, Davis & Company compound a drug under sterile conditions. *Parke, Davis Photo*

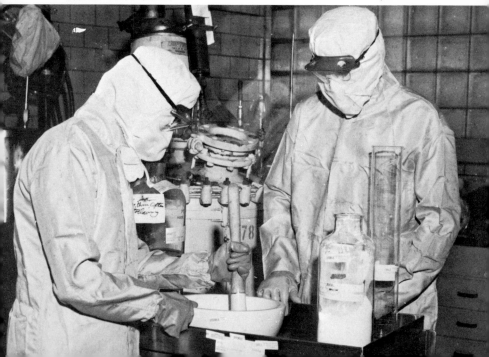

Squibb Division personnel fill cylinders with an antibiotic that has been mixed by revolving the large triangular-shape metal container. The entire area is controlled by exacting sterile techniques.

Tablet processing plant of Geigy Chemical Corporation, Suffern, N.Y. Some products require 75 coats. *Geigy Chemical Corp.*

From this stark room, a 20-year-old California youth leaped three stories to his death while on an LSD trip. His roommate failed in his attempts to restrain the violent youth.

An FDA-BDAC agent makes an arrest at gunpoint in an undercover seizure of "bennies" and "goofballs."

FDA Photo

An FDA tea taster samples tea to determine if it is of high enough quality to be allowed into the United States.

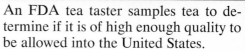

An FDA inspector checks a flour mill to see that flour is processed in sanitary fashion, and that building, storage facilities and machinery are properly maintained.

FDA Photo

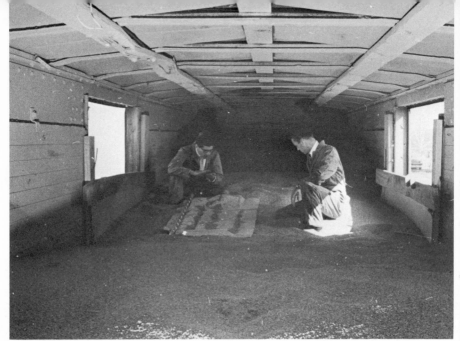

FDA inspectors take samples from carload of grain for laboratory examination to detect possible rodent or insect filth or other contamination. Bits of insect wings, hair, etc., are detected and identified by microscopic examination. *FDA Photo*

FDA inspector sifts flour in flour mill for on-the-spot contamination check. He will take samples to laboratory for thorough analysis. *FDA Photo*

This laboratory balance scale weighs accurately in thousandths of grams.
FDA Photo

A lab technician uses separation process for further examination of chemical components.

FDA Photo

FDA Photo

FDA inspector takes sampling of imported olives for laboratory examination as to quality, contamination, etc.

Smith, Kline & French Laboratories experts obtain an electro-cardiogram from a trained dog in delicate blood pressure studies.   *Smith, Kline & French Photo*

In a beer-bottling plant, an FDA inspector checks for general cleanliness, harmful additives in the beer and proper labeling.   *FDA Photo*

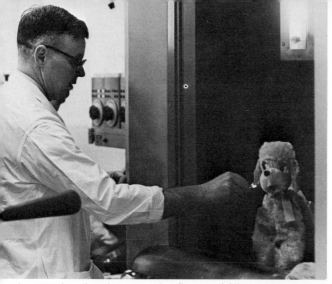

An FDA scientist tests the flammability of a stuffed toy. If considered hazardous to children, such toys can be banned from interstate commerce. *FDA Photo*

An FDA scientist measures colors in FDA's color certification program.

FDA Photo

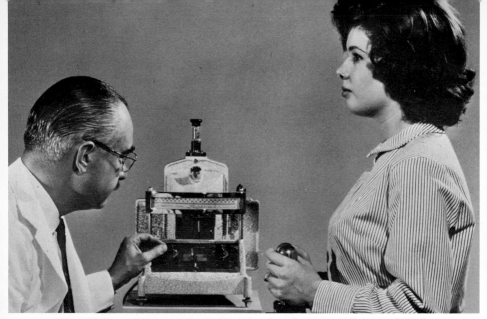

The "Micro-Dynameter." Hundreds of these "diagnostic" devices were seized by the FDA as worthless.

FDA Photo

Under supervision of Army gunnery experts, FDA-BDAC agents must maintain high standards in use of firearms. *FDA Photo*

though this was only a few days after a previous fifty had been purchased on prescription.

Families of dangerous-drug users may often suffer, too. Dr. Joel Fort, director of the Center for Treatment and Education on Alcoholism, in Oakland, California, quoted a letter he received from a Los Angeles woman. She wrote: "The experience of living with a barbiturate addict is a hell in which you wander helplessly, receiving little or no help from the medical profession. Why don't you doctors *think* when you prescribe pills? Probably a pill is the easiest way out for you—but how about the families who bear the later burden?"

Since 1966 the solving of numerous cases involving illegal use of barbiturates and other drugs of abuse has been directly due to the efficient work of BDAC agents, whose training and experience are geared to their unique law-enforcement duties. Officially they are classed by the U. S. Civil Service Commission as criminal investigators, but in addition to standard criminal investigation techniques the agents are trained in such problems as: drug identification; suppressing counterfeit drugs; drug accountability; social and psychological theories of criminal behavior; and the rehabilitation of drug abusers.

Training sessions last for six weeks and cover a wide subject range. United States attorneys may speak about arrest and search problems; reports are discussed and criticized; representatives from various Federal or state offices lecture on questions related to drug abuse. Each agent gets training in weapons, attends regular target practice sessions at a firing range and must maintain specified levels of shooting proficiency to qualify for carrying a gun. He is taught methods of self-defense, including judo and karate.

Many BDAC agents have already had valuable experience in other law-enforcement agencies. Some are former FDA inspectors, some have been investigators in the Department of Labor, the Internal Revenue Service, the Federal Bureau of Narcotics, the U. S. Secret Service, the FBI or in city police departments.

A few new agents have just come from college. All are college graduates, for the BDAC agent must be an accountant, a criminal investigator, a counselor, a sociologist and a psychologist. He must understand the motivations of people, particularly the youths who fall prey first to drug experimentation and then to drug habits.

John Finlator, director of the Bureau of Drug Abuse Control, is proud of his men and their accomplishments. "The BDAC agent," he says, "must cross back and forth to the worlds of the legitimate and the illegitimate—from the upper world of drug commerce to the underworld of drug abuse. It takes a special kind of person to do that. It takes a BDAC agent."

One of the BDAC's major drug-abuse problems involves the distribution, sale, and use of LSD-25, the hallucinogenic drug that sends thousands of young people on psychedelic "trips"—some of which end at a very final destination, death.

7

LSD: Ticket To Tragedy

ARTHUR was nineteen years old, Frank was twenty. They shared a small apartment three floors up in a New York brownstone. One afternoon in their living room, Frank ate a sugar cube containing LSD-25.

He sat quietly for a little while, then jumped up and knocked over a chair. "I'm going to Europe!" he cried. "I'm going to Europe and get my girl! You hear? I'm going to Europe!" He kicked the chair.

"Okay, Frankie boy, okay," Arthur said. "But you can't go right now. You have to pack and everything. Just sit down for a minute." Gently he led Frank toward the sofa. Frank plopped down and put both hands on the sides of his head, resting his elbows on his knees. In a few moments he sat up and laughed wildly, then began to cry. Sobbing, he looked up at Arthur and said, "What's happening? What place is this?"

A few minutes later he rose quickly and rushed toward the apartment entrance. Arthur grabbed him by one arm and tried to calm him as they struggled. Suddenly Frank stood still, squinted at his roommate and said, "What's going on? Where am I, anyway?"

"You're home, Frankie, right here at home. Just take it easy, now, take it easy."

Frank began to walk across the room slowly. He turned and glanced at Arthur. He began to talk incoherently, gesturing with both arms. Then, without warning, he dashed into the bedroom, slammed and locked the door. An instant later Arthur heard the horrible crash of breaking glass and broke into the bedroom. A few jagged pieces of the window stuck out of the sides of the frame. Arthur rushed to look out. On the pavement, three stories below, beside an upset trash can lay the twisted body of his friend. Frank had taken a "trip"— but to Eternity, not to Europe.

Scrawled in sizable capital letters on the walls of the bedroom were the words "SEX, LOVE, SENSITIVITY."

Frank's tragic death was due directly to LSD and the hallucinations it generated in his mind. LSD begins with ergot, a fungus that grows on rye and wheat. In the Middle Ages, people who ate grain that had been contaminated with ergot became victims of madness and also suffered from an acute skin infection called St. Anthony's fire, now known as erysipelas.

Drug manufacturers use ergot in the production of drugs such as ergotine, which contracts body tissues, and ergotamine, helpful in treating migraine headaches. In the chemical breakdown of ergot, lysergic acid is produced, and lysergic acid is the base of LSD. These three letters, in fact, are de-

rived from the full name of the drug—lysergic acid diethylamide.

There are other dangerous hallucinogens. Mescaline, a
chemical taken from peyote, a Mexican cactus, has long been
used by various Indian tribes in religious ceremonies. This,
somewhat like the use of wine in the Christian and Jewish
religions, has never been considered a problem.

An extract made from mushrooms found in Central America has also been used in primitive ceremonials. It's called
psilocybin.

Another member of the hallucinogenic group is dimethyltryptamine, or DMT. It can be made synthetically or from
certain kinds of plant seeds found in South America, where
some Indian tribes make a powder from the seeds and inhale
it like snuff.

Of all these hallucinogens, LSD is the best known, the
widest used, the most powerful, and presents the greatest
threat to health and life. It is dangerous in exceedingly small
amounts. As little as 100 micrograms (a speck little larger
than the period at the end of this sentence) can produce hallucinations that may last for hours or days, that can distort
and magnify one's senses, create violent impulses, vary widely
from person to person, and that may recur weeks or months
later without the drug's being taken again.

One Los Angeles boy who took LSD was killed while
walking on the freeway, convinced that he was invisible to
everyone.

A young man in Brooklyn murdered his wife's mother
while he was under the influence of LSD, but when the
effects of the drug wore off, he was horror-stricken and unable to remember any reason for the killing.

An English girl in London, high on LSD, believed she could "fly" to the United States, leaped from a window and was killed by the fall.

These and other deaths were caused directly or indirectly by LSD, because the drug removes the victim's natural self-preservation instincts, sensible judgment or his ability to recognize common dangers.

Dr. Jean Paul Smith of the BDAC has pointed out that the effects of hallucinogenic drugs have been studied for many years. In 1888 Louis Lewin, a pioneer in such studies, reported to scientific groups on the effects of peyote and similar drugs. In 1938 LSD was made synthetically by Dr. Albert Hofman and Dr. Arthur Stoll in the laboratories of Sandoz, the Swiss pharmaceutical firm. In 1943 Dr. Hofman accidentally swallowed a small amount of the drug and later made this entry in his journal:

> I noted with dismay that my environment was undergoing progressive change. Everything seemed strange and I had the greatest difficulty in expressing myself. My visual fields wavered and everything appeared deformed as in a faulty mirror. I was overcome by a feeling that I was going crazy, the worst part of it being that I was clearly aware of my condition. The mind and power of observation were apparently unimpaired.

According to Dr. Smith, "After ingestion of LSD no immediate change may be noticed. Although there is no definite sequence or series of invariable effects of LSD, certain types of changes are typical. From twenty to forty-five minutes later there may be an experience of visual changes where objects unexpectedly begin to move. Feeling may become more intense and rapid changes in mood may occur. The subject may become extremely emotional, with uncontrolled laughing or crying. He may or may not be responsive to his environment, and meaningful communication with him may prove difficult. Intensified and distorted sensations of touch are most frequent, and illusory phenomena are found more often than true hallucinations. When they do occur, hallucinations may overwhelm the individual, especially if panic and an intense feeling of losing one's mind accompany them."

Dr. Smith also says that time judgment under LSD is impaired and that time may seem to slow down or stand still. The victim's image of his own body may change so that he no longer feels the parts of his body or limbs connected in the usual way.

Other disturbing physical effects were described by Jack Bologna of the BDAC. "There's an increase in blood pressure and heart rate; the blood sugar goes up; there may be nausea, chills, flushes, irregular breathing, sweating of the hands and trembling of the arms and legs," he said. "Sleep is virtually impossible until at least eight to ten hours after the LSD episode is over. The pupils of the eyes are widely dilated, so that dark glasses are often worn, even at night, for protection against the light."

Frequently persons who use LSD also use other dangerous drugs, including amphetamines and marijuana. (Cases involving marijuana are within the investigative jurisdiction of the Federal Bureau of Narcotics.) Users of LSD and the other hallucinogens are found mostly among "beatniks" and "hippies," and occasionally on college campuses. As Mr. Bologna pointed out, some use it for "kicks," some because they are rebellious, some because they are intellectually curious—

but all are courting grave danger to their minds and bodies by such experimentation.

There was a time when LSD was used in the United States for legitimate experimental investigations under tight controls. In 1953 Sandoz Pharmaceuticals, on its own initiative, approached the FDA to discuss clinical investigations it was planning to pursue in America. At that time LSD was considered a "new drug," and the FDA agreed it could be distributed only to qualified research psychiatrists for use solely as an investigational drug. For ten years, from 1953 to 1963, experiments with LSD took place in this country, as well as in Europe.

In 1962 the Kefauver-Harris Drug Amendments modified the definition of a "new drug" and required that a drug be both effective and safe before it could be marketed commercially. The studies of LSD had failed to establish its safety or efficacy. In June, 1963, the FDA issued new regulations for "new drug" investigations, requiring that a sponsor must file with the FDA an experimentation program that was reasonably safe and responsibly conducted.

Sandoz Pharmaceuticals filed a basic plan for testing LSD under the new regulations. Eventually, about seventy researchers received LSD and were sponsored by Sandoz.

Meantime (since about 1960) the illegal production, distribution and use of LSD began to skyrocket. Researchers at Harvard University gave the drug to students outside a proper research setting, and this practice spread until, by cultural diffusion, a "drug spirit" slowly developed. It was spurred on by publicity and by "cause seekers," who came to view LSD as a symbol of protest against cultural values held by society at large.

Public reaction began to mount. Congress conducted extensive hearings into the abuse of hallucinogenic and other drugs, then passed the Drug Abuse Control Amendments in 1965 to establish controls over the depressants, stimulants and hallucinogens. Penalties were provided to reduce illegal traffic and control supplies of these drugs. Possession of LSD is not a Federal crime, but selling, giving or distributing LSD is unlawful, and violators are subject to imprisonment for one year or a $1,000 fine, or both.

In April, 1966, Sandoz Pharmaceuticals withdrew its sponsorship of investigations using LSD. As the only legal producer of the drug, Sandoz transferred its entire remaining LSD stock (about 22 grams) to the National Institute of Mental Health (NIMH). As of 1968, the only *legal* supply of LSD in the United States for clinical research on humans is either at NIMH or in the possession of a few investigators approved to continue their studies. LSD is not manufactured legally anywhere in the United States, and the abuse of the drug is entirely dependent upon homemade ("bathtub") LSD, or supplies smuggled into the country from foreign sources.

Smuggling of LSD is very hard to detect. A small packet inside an ordinary letter from abroad could contain ten thousand doses. A small box of face powder brought through customs could easily contain 150,000 doses of LSD. At the user level, one dose has a potential sale value of five dollars. At this rate, one kilogram (2.2 pounds) of LSD would theoretically be worth about $50 million.

Other interesting information about LSD comes from the Division of Case Assistance, BDAC.

"LSD, depending upon its purity, is a white-to-tan-colored

powderlike substance," one expert explains. "When dissolved in water, the resulting solution is colorless, odorless and tasteless. LSD is also soluble in alcohol and contributes no color, odor or taste to the solution. Because of this, the manner and methods by which LSD is illegally transported and sold are unlimited. In the early days of the illicit traffic, LSD was usually placed on sugar cubes when sold to the user. Soon, however, the possession of sugar cubes became synonymous with the possession of LSD."

After the sugar cube came the LSD capsule. The LSD was mixed, or "cut," with baking powder, lactose or other easy-to-obtain powders. The mixture was then colored with various food dyes and placed in gelatin capsules. Again, the capsules became synonymous with LSD use.

"Since then," the expert says, "the objects used by both peddlers and users to replace the sugar cubes and capsules have become more and more imaginative. LSD has been found on such common items as animal crackers, hard candy and candy mints, wafers, suckers, chewing gum, aspirin, vitamins, antacid tablets, blotter paper, stationery, handkerchiefs, postage stamps, beads and other costume jewelry. One LSD user claimed to have smuggled LSD into jail with him by painting it on his fingernails."

Some illegal wholesalers handled LSD in liquid form. Vodka LSD became popular. The wholesaler figured how much LSD should be dissolved in a bottle of vodka so that a single drop of the mixture represented one dose. Some wholesalers simply dissolved LSD in distilled water and sold the liquid in eye-dropper bottles. Supplies of liquid LSD were often disguised by added coloring and by being poured into empty bottles that had held mouthwash, shaving lotion or other household or toilet items.

What sort of people use LSD? The answer seems to be: all sorts. Dr. Donald B. Louria, head of the Infectious Disease Laboratory at Bellevue Hospital, New York City, and associate professor of medicine, Cornell University Medical College, gathered some interesting data as the result of admissions to Bellevue Hospital. Here are some of his findings:

SOME CHARACTERISTICS OF 114 LSD USERS:

Average age	23 (range 15 to 43)
Male	68.4%
White	88.4%
LSD 1 to 3 times only	72.8%
Overwhelming panic	13.1%
Violence	12.3%
Homicidal or suicidal	8.6%
Underlying overt mental disease	34.2%
Required extended hospitalization	15.8%

OCCUPATIONAL HISTORY, 68 CASES:

Student		15
	High School	6
	College or graduate	9
Unemployed		12
Writer, artist, musician, photographer		11
Cook, waiter, caterer		7
Welder, carpenter, printer		5
Model, dancer		5
Physician, engineer, pharmacist		4
Sociologist, teacher		4
Typist, beautician		2
Housewife		2
Rancher		1

In Los Angeles, California, BDAC agents found that LSD was not used as widely by college students as had sometimes been reported. In college *towns,* yes, but not necessarily among college students. Of 191 arrests for dangerous drug violations made during one year in Berkeley, only six involved students—the majority were simply "hangers-on to the academic scene." The FDA says, "We can reasonably estimate that student *experimentation* may run as high as 15 percent if we include *all* hallucinogens."

In about nine of every ten BDAC investigations of drug abuse, whatever the drug under suspicion, agents have found that marijuana was also involved. Many LSD users also smoke marijuana, and it has been established that numerous narcotics pushers and addicts sell LSD to get money with which to buy heroin, marijuana or other narcotics. For this reason, a working agreement exists between the BDAC and the Federal Bureau of Narcotics, and agents of both bureaus work in close cooperation not only with each other, but also with state and local enforcement agencies.

Users of LSD buy supplies of the drug that are made in crude laboratories with dirty equipment, often in filthy surroundings. The clandestine manufacturer cares nothing about the purity or safety of his product—his primary concern is to stay in business. The result is that his black market customers may often use LSD that is heavily contaminated and of varying strength, thus adding to the physical harm it can cause.

An offshoot of the LSD problem concerns the illegal production and use of methamphetamine ("meth"), a drug that has legitimate medicinal value as a suppressant of appetite in the treatment of overweight patients. Among hippies and others, the drug is known as "speed," and the more intelligent hippies ("diggers") coined a slogan, "Meth is Death."

In 1967 some of the underground hippie newspapers and

magazines boomed meth as a drug that produced bizarre reactions. Some users found that if they took enough speed, it
produced hallucinations, but that a tolerance developed
quickly and each dose had to be larger than the one before.
The users (they're called "speed freaks") would therefore
take the drug in increasing quantities for eight to twelve
days consecutively, ignoring the fact that it acted not only to
destroy their desire for food, but also to stimulate and excite
them so that they felt no need for sleep. At the end of their
"trip," having gone without food or sleep for one to two
weeks, they collapsed. As an aftermath, many developed a
type of schizophrenia characterized by stupor, muscular rigid-
ity and occasional mental agitation, and couldn't even be
reached by psychiatric treatment. In San Francisco some
hippies have warned newcomers that "Meth is Death" and
to beware of speed.

One unusual episode should be mentioned here, because
it concerns a teenager who was given official permission to
use LSD—but not on himself. A seventeen-year-old boy in
Decatur, Georgia, as a science project, fed small amounts of
LSD to common garden spiders and studied their web con-
struction before and after they took the drug. Spiders whose
normal webs were beautifully symmetrical spun webs in odd
and crazy patterns after their LSD trips.

The supply of LSD used by the student was kept under
lock and key by the boy's father, who also closely supervised
the experiments. The boy won a Science Fair prize, received
the Award of the Year from the Georgia Power Company,
and was given a special award by the FDA.

Jack Bologna of the BDAC has made some significant observations concerning drug abuse and abusers. "Today," he

points out, "every writer on the subject of values says they are changing at a rapid rate. For young people trying to find their place in the world, the change is undoubtedly more traumatic than it is for the older generation. The traditional values at stake seem to be traditional religious beliefs, the value of hard work and 'delayed reward,' simple patriotism, chastity in sexual relations and the heroes and accomplishments of former times. I think you'll find that each of these has been challenged seriously by writers, even in popular articles and books.

"The newer values," he goes on, "have been classed together by some as the Cult of Experience—that is, experience for its own sake. Some of these are the emphasis on adventure, sincerity and responsiveness, close personal relations, individualism and an interest in nature and the arts. One part of this new cult that seems to grate on the older generation is the emphasis on immediate pleasure, or pleasure and activity unrelated to future benefits. Very prominent in the minds of both its proponents and detractors is sexual freedom."

But doesn't a part of the new cult fit in with the older American values? "Yes," says Bologna. "Individualism, sincerity, friendship and appreciation of nature are certainly compatible. The forms that these values take—the beards and sandals, for example—may annoy elders, but the values they serve aren't really offbeat. Much of the repugnance we feel toward drug taking, with or without sex, is probably tied to our rejection of the idea of pleasure for the sake of pleasure alone, more than any other new value. We tend to feel that pleasure ought to be associated with other ends: good food is okay in the context of sociability; an enjoyable swim or walk keeps us in condition; and so on. I think we *should* discredit immediate pleasure that may be detrimental to health or future stability, and drug use is dangerous on this count. Perhaps in confrontations of the older and younger generations, we should be careful to make this point rather than to indict pleasure itself."

His conclusion: "Our best advice to young people may be to choose the best among the new and the old values, but not to reject the whole package on either side. Some of the new may be unavoidable and even necessary as an antidote to social ills. But some of the old cannot be cast aside with impunity. One of our oldest values is conservation of body and mind. Health is a strong tenet in the major religions of the West, and in some of the Eastern ones, too. For the sake of the species, let's hope that it will be retained."

8

Label Lures and
Phony Cures

A NOTICE issued by the FDA called public attention to a hormone preparation called Liefcort, allegedly beneficial in the treatment of arthritis. This product, said the FDA, was developed and promoted by a fugitive from justice who had fled to Canada when he was sought by United States marshals to answer charges of selling a "cure" for baldness.

A seventy-one-year-old California woman who suffered from arthritis read a magazine article about Liefcort, flew to Canada and bought a year's supply, which she brought back to the United States. Two months later, after taking the "medicine," she was hospitalized because of internal bleeding. After an operation to halt the bleeding, she developed pneumonia and died.

Liefcort had not been released by the FDA as a new drug. The public warning stated that the facts available about the manufacture of the drug and the lack of laboratory control to insure its composition and safety were such that its use, even for experimental purposes, was hazardous.

Liefcort is in the FDA category of "misbranded and adulterated drugs." As explained by the FDA, "Stepped-up operations under the 1962 Kefauver-Harris Drug Amendments brought the problem of drug misbranding into an entirely new focus. In the past it was necessary for the government to establish in court that claims for effectiveness in the treatment or prevention of disease were false and misleading. Now effectiveness must be established by the sponsor *before* a new drug is approved for marketing, as well as for drugs previously permitted to be marketed under the 1938–1962 new-drug provisions."

The medical quack of every age tries to capitalize on the latest scientific advances. Electricity, electronics and atomic energy have each in their turn launched pseudoscientific promotions.

One day two FDA inspectors were returning to their Minneapolis headquarters from a corn-cannery inspection when they noticed a new sign in a field along the highway. The sign pointed down a side road and called attention to a "uranium treatment center" for arthritics. Sufferers from arthritis, cancer and chronic diseases are prime prey for the medical charlatan.

The FDA men drove to the town mentioned on the sign and made a number of inquiries about the new enterprise, but no one seemed to know about it. Finally a filling-station operator said that he had noticed some unusual activity in an old store that had been empty for a long time.

At the old store the inspectors found two young brothers busily painting and refurbishing the place, together with adjacent living quarters. The store had about twenty new cots installed in a hospital-type ward. Each cot bore ten or twelve plastic pillows filled with a brown sandy substance which the brothers described as "uranium ore."

The brothers were recent college graduates who had read about the financial success of certain "uranium tunnels" (in which patients, for a fee, sat quietly for effects of the uranium to cure their ills). Their plan apparently was to have patients lie on the plastic pillows as a treatment for arthritis.

"It was evident," says the FDA, "that the brothers didn't really believe in the effectiveness of their ore as a medical treatment, but they did fervently believe in separating anyone from his hard-earned cash. They readily admitted transporting the uranium to Minnesota from a western state in their privately owned automobile, but refused to sign an affidavit to that effect when the inspectors informed them that they were about to launch an illegal venture by making false and misleading claims for a so-called 'drug' that had crossed interstate lines."

The brothers indignantly demanded to know the name of the supervisor of the FDA men. Next day they made an appointment to see the supervisor. Ultimately they withdrew from the business before it even opened. The two FDA inspectors were their first and only "customers."

Someone has said that medical quacks are "men with hearts of stone, souls without conscience, and well-filled bank accounts." The FDA points out that the quack sells the most precious commodity in the world—*hope*. His targets are usually victims of painful incurable diseases, and hypochondriacs, seeking treatment for imaginary ailments. The quack's allies are anxiety, pain, depression, fear and hopelessness.

Arthritis offers special opportunities to the quack, because at least twelve million Americans suffer from some form of this painful affliction. In testifying before a Senate Subcommittee on Frauds Affecting the Elderly, a San Francisco woman said, "If we fall for the phony—and sooner or later most of us do—it's because the pains of arthritis are something that you just can't describe. Because nobody knows why it comes or how or when it goes."

This same witness told about her experiences with unorthodox practitioners during private investigations she conducted in and near California. Among treatments recommended to her was one calling for the drinking of "alfalfa tea" and plunging her hands into hot and cold water. Another was the use of a box containing "numerous little bottles with lavender caps" over which a little transparent crystal ball was swung. She was told that another woman got a "successful treatment" simply by calling a certain doctor on the telephone!

Many arthritis victims agree with one of the statements expressed by the witness: "There must be an exchange list of arthritis victims, because if you get on one list you receive material advertising all manner of devices—items such as vibrators, whirlpool baths, salves, uranium mitts and things of that sort."

Mr. Jerry Walsh, special educational consultant to the Arthritis and Rheumatism Foundation, testified before the subcommittee. Within three weeks after his appearance, fellow arthritis sufferers sent him 4,137 letters recommending 231 products ranging in price from two dollars to two hundred dollars, including many "cures" and "lasting remedies."

The Senate subcommittee estimated roughly that arthritic quackery robs sufferers in the United States of some $250 million a year.

In the 1950's and early 1960's, hundreds—perhaps thousands—of men and women sought cures for their various ills from Roy F. Paxton, the balding, middle-aged secretary-treasurer of Millpax, Inc., manufacturer of Millrue "tonic." Many of his customers seemed to believe that Paxton was saving the whole human race from the effects of cancer, ulcers, kidney and bladder troubles and a host of other diseases.

Millrue was advertised as "nature's own." Says the FDA, "It was nature's own, all right. Its prime ingredient was mallow, a tall slender weed that grows in swamps. It has no pharmaceutical significance of any kind."

What Paxton was manufacturing and promoting for cancer treatment, according to the FDA, was an eight-ounce bottle containing a liquid mixture of water, vitamins, ferric ammonium citrate and mallow extractives. The front label of the tinted bottle bore a portrait of Paxton in a doctor's white coat and described the contents as an "iron tonic, a hematonic and a stomachic." It claimed to increase the hemoglobin of the blood, and it carried the words, "Registered in the U. S. Patent Office No. 632,557." It listed the simple ingredients in grams and milligrams and carried a modest little line, "An effective tonic for simple anemia. We don't make any further claims."

Paxton and Millrue made no further printed claims on the label—but insert leaflets and advertising for Millrue carried a crest and this verse:

132

"Millrue is here for you,
It's made folks feel much better, too.
Millrue is nature's own,
It's made of herbs that God has grown.
If you feel life's not worth while
Won't you give Millrue a trial?
Don't feel bad—don't feel blue,
Try Millrue—Try Millrue."

Although no printed claims for efficacy in curing cancer, heart disease or tumors appeared anywhere, extensive use was made of testimonial letters from users of Millrue, stating how the mixture had cured them of cancer, heart trouble and other serious ailments.

To FDA officials this constituted "misbranding." Misbranded samples were collected, and in July, 1958, a criminal prosecution was filed in the Federal court at Springfield, Illinois, against Millpax, Inc., and Roy F. Paxton. At first the defendants pleaded not guilty, but after learning of the extent of the government's case, they entered a plea of guilty three months later. Paxton and his company were fined $1,235, which was promptly paid.

Soon Paxton gave himself another medical degree and continued to use Millrue in examining and treating people for diabetes, high blood pressure, ulcers, arthritis, tumors, cancer and other diseases. Again the FDA acted. This time the charge was "inadequate directions for use." In April, 1961, a Federal grand jury in Springfield, Illinois, indicted Paxton and the company. They pleaded not guilty and elected to fight the case in court. The same judge presided. The trial began October 30 and ended November 2, 1961, when a jury found Paxton and the corporation guilty as charged.

A charge of "second offense" was proved November 8, 1962. Three months later Paxton was sentenced to six years in prison, with three years' probation to begin upon completion of his sentence. In addition, he and his corporation were fined $7,000. The conviction was appealed, but the Seventh Court of Appeals upheld it. Conviction on the third count was dismissed, and the jail sentence for Paxton was reduced from six to three years. Total fines were reduced from $7,000 to $4,000.

Millrue cropped up in another case involving Will H. Roberts, a house painter who set up a "health center." Roberts was fined for misbranding Millrue, soy-germ oil tablets and alfalfa tablets as cures for cancer, black cancer, inoperable cancer, lung cancer, malignant cysts, arthritis, piles and other diseases. In suspending a two-year jail sentence, the judge told Roberts that the age of black magic was over, and that if he advertised a cure even for athlete's foot he would have to serve the two years. The judge was particularly indignant that Roberts had advertised he could counteract the harmful effects of thalidomide.

Another important case that received national publicity concerned an alleged cancer remedy known as Krebiozen.

Krebiozen was a whitish powder supposedly derived from the blood of horses. Involved in its distribution were Dr. Andrew C. Ivy, Dr. William F. P. Phillips, Dr. Stevan Durovic and his brother, Marko Durovic, all of Chicago, Illinois.

In 1963 FDA inspectors discovered that Krebiozen had not been made as its promoters claimed. Following the procedure described by Stevan Durovic for the production of Krebiozen from horses' blood, FDA scientists learned that the procedure did not work and that no so-called Krebiozen powder could be produced in the way Durovic claimed it had been produced.

Although Krebiozen was promoted and sold as a cancer remedy, records required by regulations for the investigative use of drugs were not available to the FDA. The sponsors were told on January 31, 1963, that if they were to continue interstate distribution of the drug for investigational use, under the Kefauver-Harris Drug Amendments they must submit before June 7 their plan for continued investigational use. This would include information on how Krebiozen was made and controlled, its toxicity and the results from past clinical investigations.

An application for investigational use of Krebiozen was filed June 6, 1963, with a proposal that the investigational work be done by the National Cancer Institute, but without the required information about composition, toxicity and controls. This application was voluntarily withdrawn by the sponsors on July 12, 1963, which automatically made it illegal for them to continue interstate distribution of Krebiozen.

The sponsors tried to prevent further FDA investigation by bringing an injunction suit aimed at lifting the ban on interstate shipments of the drug. The suit was subsequently dismissed.

FDA scientists, with the help of university and other outside consultants, analyzed a sample furnished by Stevan Durovic and Dr. Ivy as pure Krebiozen. They found it to be creatine, a common laboratory chemical. These scientists also analyzed Krebiozen ampules, ready for injection into patients, and found them to contain only mineral oil, sometimes with a small amount of a creatine derivative and an alcohol.

The sponsors submitted to the National Cancer Institute the records of a selected group of 504 patients treated with Krebiozen. In August, 1963, the institute appointed a committee of twenty-four of the nation's foremost cancer experts to review the claimed "cures" and "effective treatments." Because the material provided by the Krebiozen Research Foundation was inadequate for scientific evaluation, the FDA undertook the collection of complete medical records of all the cases submitted by the foundation. The committee of experts, after a detailed review of these records, concluded unanimously that Krebiozen had no anticancer effect whatever. In October the National Cancer Institute accepted the committee's recommendation against clinical testing of the drug.

While this evaluation was being conducted, FDA scientists and expert consultants demonstrated that the product identified as Krebiozen powder by the sponsors was not a tissue hormone, as claimed, but was actually creatine monohydrate, a normal component of the human body. The chemical had been tested previously against animal tumors by the National Cancer Institute and found ineffective, even in high doses.

Continued analyses of samples of Krebiozen ampules by the FDA showed that those shipped before 1960 contained nothing but mineral oil, while ampules shipped since then contained mineral oil plus minute amounts of amyl alcohol and a derivative of creatine that was soluble in mineral oil.

Among the claims made by the sponsors was one that the cost of producing a single gram of Krebiozen was $17,000. The FDA says, "It is in fact a common chemical worth about thirty cents per gram."

Another claim was that a certain man who had used Krebiozen was now healthy. The FDA found that the man had died of cancer eight years earlier.

The government has said since 1961 that it was prepared to make a test of Krebiozen if presented with any scientific data that would justify such a test. In collecting the data to determine whether a test was justified, the FDA found that "there was no such thing as Krebiozen as an anticancer agent, and that the promoters of the drug had been victimizing cancer patients into buying ampules of mineral oil."

On November 17, 1964, a Federal grand jury indicted the Durovic brothers, Dr. Ivy and Dr. Phillips on forty-nine counts of conspiracy, mail fraud, mislabeling and making false statements to the government about Krebiozen. The Internal Revenue Service claimed in April, 1965, that the Durovic brothers owed the government $929,157 in back taxes on profits from their Chicago medical laboratory which produces Krebiozen.

Trial of the FDA case began on April 28, 1965. On January 31, 1966, the four defendants were acquitted on the criminal charges, but the scientific data of 1963 establishing that Krebiozen was not a treatment for cancer was not overturned by the jury. The FDA says it is determined to keep Krebiozen out of interstate commerce, but the drug is still legally available within the state of Illinois.

Evidence presented at the trial established that some patients accepted Krebiozen as a cancer treatment, instead of

X rays or surgery, and thus allowed their disease to progress beyond control.

Under the law a new drug may not be distributed in interstate commerce unless it has been approved as safe and effective. Says the FDA, "Krebiozen has never been approved, and it does not now meet the standards for distribution, even for investigational use. Cancer patients and their families should be warned not to risk their lives or to throw their money away on this worthless drug. FDA will carry out its responsibility to the public by doing whatever will be necessary to keep Krebiozen out of interstate commerce. We will do this as a life-saving activity. Each day a person with treatable cancer relies upon Krebiozen is a day that brings him closer to death."

Even in the face of such warnings, many people may continue to use products that have little or no healing powers, but in which ailing men and women place their faith and sometimes a last desperate hope. These products are not only potions, pills and powders—many of them are gadgets and gimmicks, and some would be laughable if they didn't do so much harm.

9____

Gadgets and Gimmicks

A NEWSPAPER advertisement for a device called Crampeze started FDA inspectors on an investigation. Crampeze turned out to be a clear plastic bag similar to those used to hold vegetables in a supermarket. It was promoted to relieve pains of foot and leg cramps.

Directions for its use were rather fantastic. They called for breathing into the bag by exhaling through the mouth, then inhaling the bagged breath through the nostrils. The process was to be repeated five times, and if the cramps persisted, treatment was to be repeated for five nights.

The inspectors found that a huge number of the breather bags had been made and that a massive distribution campaign was just about to begin. The bags had been manufactured locally, but were made from plastic crystals that had traveled in interstate commerce, so the raw material and all stocks of the bags were seized.

Another quack device stopped by the FDA before it could victimize gullible people was the Rado Pad—simply a quantity of plain crushed rock packaged in feather-ticking cloth. The pads came in three sizes selling for seven-fifty, fifteen and thirty dollars each. They were accompanied by pamphlets claiming that they were beneficial for treating arthritis, rheumatism, sinus and muscular ailments. FDA inspectors visited the firm and found that an automobile load of the pads had just arrived, and that the first pad had not yet been sold. A sample was collected, and the dealer was ordered to withhold sale. Soon afterwards the owner abandoned the pads and skipped town. The pads were seized.

Quackery thrives on ignorance, despair, superstition and fear. It uses misinformation to arouse false hopes. It takes advantage of man's gullibility and his desire to believe the unbelievable. However, says the FDA, quackery can no longer hide under the cloak of ignorance, because science is now capable of distinguishing the effective from the ineffective. The FDA fights quackery in a two-pronged attack: (1) a vigorous enforcement program; and (2) an expanding educational and public informational program in cooperation with other governmental and private organizations, and with educational institutions.

The educational program is based on the premise that enforcement alone can't deal with quackery, because crackdowns usually come too late, after the damage has been done. FDA's long-range goal is to eliminate the basic underlying causes of quackery through education. A well-informed consumer is much less likely to make unwise choices in health products and services than the person who lacks basic knowledge in such matters. As one expert has put it, "An informed layman with a reasonable amount of common sense isn't apt to trust his life to a quack."

The trouble is that not enough laymen are "informed." In one case, an injunction was issued to stop distribution of a machine called the Micro-Dynameter, a scientific-looking but worthless device that was falsely promoted for diagnosing or curing many diseases and conditions. Thousands of patients were hoodwinked into believing that they had diseases they didn't have when these machines were used for "diagnoses," and others failed to get proper treatment for diseases they actually had. More than eleven hundred of the devices were seized by the government or voluntarily destroyed by health practitioners.

The FDA scientists found that Micro-Dynameter simply measured the amount of perspiration on the user's skin. The device sold for $875, or the cost to patients was five to ten dollars per treatment. On this basis, if the machines seized by the FDA had continued in use, they would have brought their operators from $25 to $50 million.

In January, 1963, more than a hundred Hubbard E-meters and Hubbard Electrometers were seized, along with three tons of associated literature, in possession of an organization called the Founding Church of Scientology. The FDA says this group was using the device—similar in principle to a lie detector—to screen applicants for admission to membership and then for treatment of members. After applicants had been "cleared" and treated with the instruments, according to the organization's literature, they would no longer be subject to the diseases that affect other people.

The labeling represented the devices as being helpful for such physical ailments as arthritis, cancer, stomach ulcers, radiation burns from atomic bombs, polio, the common cold and others. The seizure was challenged on the grounds that it interfered with the right of religious worship, but the court ruled this defense inadmissible, and a jury found the devices misbranded.

In the same year there were thirty-four other actions against electric gadgets, including vibrators, massage instruments, air purifiers, automobile air conditioners, negative ion generators and other instruments charged with false and misleading promotion for the prevention and cure of disease conditions. An additional fifteen seizure actions were taken against other misbranded devices such as magnetic bracelets and "affinitizers," inhalators, belts, sandals, whirlpool baths, bust developers, prosthetic devices and water softeners.

Many machines seized as being worthless for their intended use are so complicated in appearance that patients are misled into thinking the devices are scientifically designed to diagnose, treat or cure disease. Many of the machines are also too expensive (up to $2,500) for individuals to buy for home use, and look too difficult for untrained persons to operate. This helps to persuade people to pay practitioners for expensive treatments on glowing promises of their effectiveness in combating serious illnesses.

Not all quack devices look complicated or hard to operate. Among cheaper do-it-yourself treatments and cures seized were various makes of "health lamps" capable of burning the skin, jouncing contour chairs, vacuum cleaners, sacroiliac belts, foot-exercise sandals, electric sleep machines, electric wrinkle removers, several types of bath contraptions, oxygen inhalers, ozone generators, humidifiers and a number of articles for reducing the weight and firming the skin. The de-

vices were promoted through fairs, home shows, retail stores
and in mail-order catalogues.

One company, Abunda Products, Inc., promoted a worthless device as a bust developer, which was subject to a number of seizures. Finally the company was prosecuted. Before
the criminal case came to trial, the president of the firm
changed his plea to *nolo contendere* (Latin, "I am unwilling
to contend") and consented to a decree of permanent injunction restraining shipments of the device or misbranding it
with false and misleading claims. He was sentenced to thirty
days in jail and given a one-year suspended sentence on
condition that he remain on probation for five years. In
addition he was fined $500. Investigation showed that he
and his associates had cheated unwary citizens of more than
$100,000.

In California, the government seized 560 two-inch glass
vials containing pieces of a rocklike mineral imported from
South Africa. The promoter claimed that the vial, when
worn around one's neck, gave off radiations with curative
powers for healing cancer, nervous breakdowns and ivy
poisoning.

In Olympia, Washington, seizure was made of a device
consisting of a clear plastic ball attached to a short length of
chain, which was promoted as a means of revealing the sex
of unborn children. Its promoter also claimed that it could,
by a swinging action, tell if the user were pregnant as little
as one minute after conception.

Numerous shipments of sauna baths using electrically
heated stones to produce steam in wooden cabinets were
seized on charges of misbranding by claims for reducing

body weight, preventing colds and curing sinus and other conditions.

In Detroit, Michigan, 350 electrical gadgets called the Master Violet Ray were seized for claims that they were effective in treating baldness, conditions of the throat, vagina, prostate gland, ears and nose. Claims were also made for spinal and dental treatment.

A stock of a well-known brand of foot-comfort shoes and electric foot massagers was seized in Denver, Colorado, following *oral* misbranding by a salesman who claimed that the shoes and massagers were effective for relieving all common foot troubles, removing calcium deposits in the joints, shortening muscles and curing broken-down metatarsals (foot bones).

In 1900 a man named Dinshah P. F. Ghadiali came to the United States from India and later settled in New Jersey. In the 1920's he was convicted on Mann Act (immorality) charges and served time in Atlanta Penitentiary. Subsequently he invented and promoted a notorious quack device, the Spectrochrome, which allegedly cured most diseases by rays from an ordinary light bulb shining through pieces of colored glass. The colored rays were "attuned" to body radioactive forces, and different colors supposedly cured various ailments.

Ghadiali, who became known as the colored-light man, organized a cult of ten thousand members. Training students to give treatments with his machine, he awarded them "degrees" from his "institute" and authorized them to use the letters NSC (Normalator of Spectro Chrome Metry) after their names.

The Spectrochrome sold for $475, and allegedly treated more than 150 ailments, including cancer, blindness, deafness and diabetes. To be healed, the sufferer lay nude in a darkened room during certain phases of the moon, with his head pointing north. Colored light from the Spectrochrome was aimed at afflicted areas. For example, to "cure" cancer, one moved the purple and blue slides in front of a thousand-watt bulb. To "cure" heart disease, the red and purple slides were used.

Although Ghadiali was fined and placed on probation, he continued his promotion. The FDA then obtained a permanent injunction to prohibit him from further interstate distribution of his device.

On April 29, 1966, Dinshah P. F. Ghadiali died at the age of ninety-two.

Even clothing gets into the quack act. In Chicago, FDA Inspector Susan K. Gehm posed as a potential distributor for a brassiere whose manufacturers claimed it would increase circulation, firm breast tissue, increase bust size and decrease waist size. The claims were unfounded, and the investigation resulted in the seizure of $2,700 worth of the brassieres and promotional material.

In Charlotte, North Carolina, the FDA seized a shipment of men's shorts! Manufactured in St. Petersburg, Florida, the shorts were claimed to lessen fatigue, help circulation of the blood and add years to a man's life. A large advertising placard with the words "Stop Killing Yourself" showed a robust man attired only in a pair of the shorts.

The Food, Drug and Cosmetic Act provides for removal of misbranded and adulterated drugs and dangerous devices from the market, and the prosecution of the shippers of such products. The general control of medical quackery is accomplished by routine and special investigations by the FDA field districts. Reports are submitted by the field districts to the administrative headquarters in Washington for evaluation by scientific experts, and headquarters determines whether to proceed against the articles or persons under the punitive provisions of the act.

Since many quack medical devices may be promoted or sold by mail, the Post Office Department has a direct interest in such cases, and its post-office inspectors work closely with FDA investigators to fight health quackery that involves use of the mails to defraud.

The Federal Trade Commission, whose activities are aimed at unfair trade practices and false or misleading advertising, is also a valuable ally of the FDA and the Post Office Department.

Acting on its premise that public education can help to foil the quack, the FDA, in company with the American Medical Association, sponsored the First National Congress on Medical Quackery in Washington, D. C., in 1961. This was followed by a Second National Congress in 1963. Both were designed to explore the reasons why people are vulnerable to medical quackery and how the public can be better protected. Numerous displays of quack devices gave force and color to the various talks and discussions by the participants. Through efforts such as this, through other methods of making Americans aware of the ways their health can be threatened by big-time swindlers and small-time tinkerers, the FDA, along with other Federal, state and local government regulatory agencies can and does save not only the public's money, but also lives that might otherwise be unnecessarily snuffed out.

Unfortunately, a great many people who are too intelligent to be victimized by quacks and foolish claims are amazingly careless and negligent in protecting themselves and their families in the sanctuaries of their own homes. . . .

10____

Home and Health Hazards

ON a sunny afternoon in Dallas, Texas, five teenage boys were cruising along a highway in their hot rod when the car suddenly exploded and was enveloped in a mass of flame. Three of the boys died. The other two were badly burned.

The boys had been experimenting with mixtures of model-engine fuels and other chemicals to produce souped-up effects in models. Although they usually conducted their experiments in an open field, they carried the fuel mixtures in their car. This time their luck ran out—the ingredients exploded.

FDA investigators found that many toy-engine and racing-car fuels failed to carry adequate danger warnings. The FDA took court action to remove some of these products from the market and to bring about satisfactory warning labeling on others, as required by the Federal Hazardous Substances Labeling Act (FHSLA).

This act was passed by Congress in 1960. Before that time only a dozen caustic poisons (acids and alkalis) were subject to Federal labeling requirements. Under the 1960 law, however, hazardous substances are defined as:

Articles which are toxic or highly toxic or irritant.

Articles which are flammable or extremely flammable.

Products that generate pressure through heat, decomposition or other means.

Certain radioactive materials.

Articles specifically designated as strong sensitizers. (These are so designated if the product causes injury or illness of sufficient severity and frequency to a substantial number of people, although almost any product may cause an allergic reaction in some individuals.)

The law doesn't provide for premarket clearance, but it can require the removal from consumer channels of any product that does not meet with the specific legal provisions. The FDA maintains surveillance over the labeling of approximately thirty thousand manufacturers and well over 250,000 separately trade-named, potentially hazardous products that may enter the home or workshop.

The 1960 act also requires that any potentially dangerous household product carry on its label this information:

What is in the product that makes it harmful (important information for a doctor in case the product causes injury).

How the product can hurt (flammable, harmful vapor, poison, etc.).

Special words to stress the hazard, such as DANGER,

WARNING, CAUTION—and an illustration of a skull and crossbones if the product is highly toxic.

What to do to avoid harm or injury.

What first aid to apply in case of accident (provided first aid by a layman is advisable; sometimes it isn't).

Above all, the statement: KEEP OUT OF THE REACH OF CHILDREN.

The last point is one of the most important. In California, a mother was in the bedroom with her youngest child. In another bedroom her two-year-old daughter arose from a nap and wandered into the kitchen. On the table she saw a glass jar containing a colored liquid. She thought it was fruit juice, so she drank it. It was furniture polish.

The little girl gagged. The mother heard her, rushed in and gave her first aid, then called her doctor. The child was rushed to the hospital. The doctor asked the mother for the name of the furniture polish or its ingredients, but the mother knew neither. She had borrowed the solution from a neighbor, who in turn had received it from a handyman. Although the polish was in a glass jar, the lid was not screwed down tightly, *and the jar was left where the child could reach it easily.* No one was able to find the original container or identify the ingredients. Fortunately the little victim suffered no permanent ill effects.

Another case was more tragic. In Ohio, the parents of an eighteen-month-old boy found him unconscious on the kitchen floor with an almost empty can of floor cleaner beside him. At the hospital the parents weren't sure when the boy had drunk the cleaner, but guessed that it might have been about two or three hours before they found him. He died forty-five minutes after he was admitted. The label on the can carried all the precautions required by law. In large legible type on the label were the words, "DANGER—HARMFUL OR FATAL IF SWALLOWED." Also prominent was the caution, "KEEP OUT OF THE REACH OF CHILDREN." But what good is a printed label to a child eighteen months old? If the parents had observed the warning notices, their boy would still be alive.

Children are the most frequent victims of accidental poisoning. In fact, some 90 percent of all such poisonings happen to youngsters under five years of age. The U. S. Public Health Service estimates that there are about 500,000 of these young victims every year in the United States.

The FDA states the primary reason. "The blame for the still appallingly high accidental poisoning rate must be laid at the door of a careless public, rather particularly at the door of careless parents. The information that would keep both parent and child safe—if observed—is there on the labels. We do not heed it."

Today's housewife has more chemical servants at her bidding than a houseful of genies. All sorts of cleaners and polishes stock her shelves, brighten her home and lighten her chores. Her do-it-yourself husband has a workbench with paints, paint thinners and removers, solvents, soldering compounds, fuels, perhaps radiator antifreeze or similar materials.

Many of these contain chemicals that can be dangerous in one way or another. Translated into everyday terms, the legal phrases in the FHSL Act mean that many of the familiar household products useful around the home, the basement workshop and the garage, contain chemicals that can and do inflict thousands of injuries a year. Adults and children alike inhale harmful vapors from fabric cleaners, paints, solvent finish removers, or can be burned by spilled caustics such as lyes, bleaches and rust removers.

In one sad case in Massachusetts, a baby's life could have been saved if his mother had simply read a label. The baby boy was born March 28, 1961. When he was three days old, he was circumcised, and his parents took him home. Because the attending physician wasn't available at the time they left the hospital, the parents didn't receive any direct instructions for treating the circumcision.

The doctor did, however, telephone their home and talk with the baby's grandmother. He suggested that a boric-acid *ointment* be used as a healing agent. The grandmother mistakenly thought he had suggested boric-acid *powder,* and she relayed this information to the baby's mother.

The mother sprinkled a small amount of boric-acid powder on the circumcision each time she changed the infant's diaper. She began using the powder the day she took him home and continued for a week. During this time the mother noticed that the boy's stomach seemed to be upset, so she called the doctor. He felt that the change from the hospital to the home might have been the cause, and that there was no reason for worry. Neither the mother nor the doctor thought to question the treatment being used to heal the circumcision.

The next day, however, the baby appeared quite ill, and the doctor came to see him. He found the infant dehydrated, his skin drawn tight against the skull, and his tongue heavily coated. Suspecting boric-acid poisoning, the doctor immediately sent the child to Children's Hospital in Boston. Unfortunately, the baby didn't survive the treatment and died the next day.

An autopsy later revealed symptoms of boric-acid poisoning and ten times the quantity of boric acid that could have been tolerated in the baby's liver, kidneys and skin.

The boy's mother couldn't recall reading any warning label on the can of boric-acid powder—but the label was there, and it carried these words: "WARNING: DO NOT USE AS A DUSTING POWDER, ESPECIALLY ON INFANTS, OR TAKE INTERNALLY."

Scores of children whose parents gave them candy-flavored aspirin tablets, later ate the pills like candy and became seriously ill or died, all because Mother or Dad failed to put the bottle where little hands couldn't get it.

Babies and children, of course, are not the only victims of hazardous substances. Many adults suffer serious injuries or die from poisons or other dangers, and sometimes the blame lies with the manufacturers of the hazardous products. The story of X-33 is a good example.

A Minnesota housewife was painting her basement walls with X-33, a new waterproofing paint that had just come on the market. The windows were open, no pilot lights were burning. The housewife sat down to rest. Suddenly—*boom!* A terrific explosion and flash fire blew the roof off the attached garage and turned the basement into a holocaust. The woman died two days later. Her husband, who was upstairs, was badly burned.

In Iowa, another woman was painting her basement walls with the same product. A sudden explosion and fire killed her.

In still another accident, a man was using X-33 to paint the basement walls in the home of a friend. After pouring some of the X-33 into a hand-operated pressure-type sprayer, he sprayed it on the cellar wall. About fifty feet away, in a separate room around the corner and through a doorway, there was an open-flame pilot light. Not more than sixty seconds after the man started to spray, there was a tremendous explosion. His face, neck and arms were severely burned. Investigation later showed that it was impossible for anything other than the pilot light to have ignited the fumes.

The FDA made an investigation of X-33 shortly after it came on the market. They found that it was an explosively flammable masonry waterproofer that had a flash point of 40 degrees below zero Fahrenheit. The flash point is defined as the lowest temperature at which the fumes or vapor from a liquid will ignite when exposed to a flame or spark. In other words, even in temperatures as low as 40 degrees below zero, the fumes from X-33 would ignite.

When the FDA found the dangerously low flash point, eight lots of X-33 were seized. The manufacturer was asked to recall the product from the market, or label it with adequate warnings to protect against accidents. He refused to recall the product, but did send out sticker labels to all dealers who stocked the X-33. The new labels carried stronger and more conspicuous warnings, but failed to solve the problem. Some dealers didn't even both to stick the new labels on the cans. In some cases the labels didn't stay on the containers and fell off during handling. The FDA subsequently seized twenty-one additional stocks of X-33.

Reports of explosions, fires and injuries caused by the paint fumes continued to flow into FDA offices. By late summer of

1963 the FDA concluded that the only adequate protective label for X-33 would have to be phrased in such terms that the product would probably be unsalable.

The manufacturer was given an ultimatum to relabel all outstanding stock, or face seizure of all X-33 on the market. The firm tried to forestall such seizures through a court order, but the court refused to go along with the delay. When the company continued to refuse to recall or relabel outstanding stocks of X-33, a nationwide seizure effort was begun by the FDA. Approximately six hundred seizures were made. The FDA also asked for and received help from state and local health and fire departments in tracking down X-33, and the hazard to household safety was thus removed.

An ironic sidelight to the seizure campaign occurred in Connecticut. In Federal seizures it is customary for the court to ask whether there is some salvage value to a seized product. If so, the court may give the product to a charitable institution or a government agency. When X-33 was brought into Federal court in Connecticut, a representative of one government agency asked that it be turned over to his office. He was aware only that the product had been seized because it was not properly labeled, and he knew nothing about its dangerous properties. He told the court that he intended to save the taxpayers' money by using the seized material to waterproof the basement walls of certain government buildings in Connecticut. Fortunately the FDA learned of the request, with the result that the entire stock of seized X-33 went up in smoke on the city dump.

Although the formula for X-33 was changed in July, 1963, and the flash point was raised to a much-safer 73 degrees above zero, the labels of the new and old products were hardly distinguishable from each other.

A criminal prosecution was filed against the company and its president. On June 6, 1967, the company pleaded guilty and its president pleaded *nolo contendere*. The corporation was fined $5,000, the president $2,500.

Because of the thousands of accidents to home owners and children, President Lyndon B. Johnson recommended legislation to:

Bring all hazardous substances, regardless of their wrappings, under the safeguards of the Federal Hazardous Substances Labeling Act.

Ban from interstate commerce those household substances that are so hazardous that warning labels are not adequate safeguards.

Ban the sale of toys and other children's articles containing hazardous substances, regardless of their packaging.

The 89th Congress then passed such a law, known as the Child Protection Act of 1966.

The Federal Hazardous Substances Labeling Act was exactly what its name said—a labeling law. Under the 1966 amendments, the word "labeling" was dropped from the title, and now the Hazardous Substances Act provides for consumer protection beyond that which can be realized through labeling alone.

As revised, the law makes it possible to ban household products such as X-33 from interstate commerce if the dangers warrant such a ban. The Secretary of Health, Education and Welfare can do this by issuing a regulation that classifies the article as a "banned hazardous substance." The ruling is based on a finding that, despite the labeling, the hazard to the home is so great that public health and safety can be adequately served only by keeping the product out of interstate commerce.

Before any article can be placed in this category, however, the Secretary must publish his finding in the *Federal Register*, where it is subject to comments and objections. Where the legal requirements have been fulfilled, a public hearing may take place. The law also provides procedures for review by a U. S. Circuit Court of Appeals.

If the delay caused by these procedures would involve an imminent danger to public health, the Secretary is authorized to suspend the product from the market immediately, awaiting the completion of any hearings and judicial actions.

The new amendments ban outright "any toy or other article intended for use by children which is a hazardous substance or which bears or contains a hazardous substance in such manner as to be susceptible of access by a child to whom such toy or other article is entrusted."

The need for this law was vividly illustrated on May 28, 1965, when the FDA warned parents and retailers across the country to be on the lookout for a dangerous type of imported fireworks known as crackerballs or ball-type caps (mentioned in Chapter 1). These small "torpedo" like firecrackers looked like colored candy, and were almost indistinguishable from gumdrops and certain breakfast cereals. They were sometimes sold in candy stores. In addition to exploding on impact, the balls contained an arsenic compound.

It was inevitable that children would mistake them for candy. The FDA investigated more than thirty cases in which children suffered loosened teeth, burns and cuts of the gums, tongue and cheeks. An expensive multiple-seizure campaign was required to round up an estimated sixty million cracker-balls on the market.

One importer-distributor elected to contest the seizure on the grounds that the articles were not hazardous as charged, and that the injuries they caused were innocuous. The judge upheld the government's position that the crackerball was hazardous, but ruled against FDA's claim that adequate labeling for them could not be devised. As a result, the seized goods had to be released and could be distributed under revised cautionary labels.

Under the 1966 amendments, the FDA has been able to deny recent attempts to import additional lots of crackerballs from Japan and Formosa.

Another early action by FDA under the new amendments was against certain dolls imported from Poland and England. The dolls ranged in height from seven to sixteen inches. The face was made of nitrocellulose, also known as guncotton, and burned at the rate of about one inch in three seconds. The hair was also made of a cellulose type of material that burned even faster—over two inches per second. Fortunately there were no reports of injuries, but the FDA asked the firm to recall all outstanding stocks of the dolls, and denied entry to an additional 200,000. Another 100,000 dolls were seized.

The law does permit some children's articles which, by reason of their functional purposes, require the presence of a hazardous substance. These may be exempted from the "banned" category, provided they bear appropriate warnings and are intended for children old enough to read and heed the warnings. The exemptions include such articles as chemistry sets and school supplies that may possess some degree of hazard—certain art materials, preserved biological specimens and laboratory chemicals.

The law also states that the Secretary shall exempt fireworks from the "banned-toy" classification "to the extent that he determines that they can be adequately labeled to protect the purchasers and users thereof." In considering this, the FDA decided there was no reason for banning ordinary "Class C common fireworks." Accordingly, such items as "fountains," sparklers, "torches," some skyrockets, and small firecrackers were exempted.

The exemption does *not* include cherry bombs, "salutes," and firecrackers more than 1½ inches in length and ¼ inch in diameter, and containing more than two grains of powder, nor does it include kits intended for producing explosive fireworks. Such kits, containing packets of chemicals, paper tubes and pieces of fuse, are offered for sale by mail order. Although the kits don't contain actual explosive fireworks when shipped, they have no other possible use than to make them, so these and most other types of larger explosive fireworks fall within the "banned hazardous substance" classification.

There is a proposed exemption to permit distribution of larger explosive fireworks for limited purposes, such as the firecrackers or cherry bombs used by agricultural experts to protect crops from damage by frightening off birds and other wildlife.

Fireworks such as rockets and aerial bombs, intended for public display, are not affected so long as they aren't sold for use in or around a household. If they were found in retail channels, they would be declared "banned hazardous substances," subject to seizure, and the person or persons responsible for diverting them to the general public would be liable to criminal prosecution.

In addition to the Federal ban, the various states and localities are free to restrict the distribution and sale of any fireworks that are considered illegal under state or local laws.

Another loophole in the original laws was plugged by the 1966 amendments. If products were not sold in a container or package, the government was powerless to require a warning on them, and unpackaged hazardous substances escaped seizure actions.

An example of the kind of problem this situation created was seen during Easter. Stores all over the country were selling imported toy ducklings that were potentially dangerous. These novelties were made from the stuffed skins of real ducklings and were found to contain a high concentration of benzene hexachloride, a poisonous insecticide that had been added as a preservative. Other such toys were contaminated by the *Salmonella* microorganism and still more by arsenic compounds, but since they were *not in containers* the FDA could not compel the makers to attach warnings and could not take seizure actions under the original act.

Objects made of jequirity beans (also called jumble beans) were among unpackaged articles that escaped seizure. These bright little red and black beans are pretty—and pretty deadly. One bean, chewed and swallowed, can cause death in a matter of hours. Yet many gift shops and other stores sold necklaces, swizzle sticks and other objects made of the beans.

There was no way of warning the buyers, because the items were not sold in packaged form.

The amended law requires necessary warnings to appear on the article itself, or, if this is not possible, the warnings must be placed on a sticker or tag securely fastened to the article.

As the FDA points out, "The passage of the Child Protection Act has greatly strengthened the protection afforded to the consumer by the Hazardous Substances Act. No legislation will eliminate all injuries, but these new measures go well beyond the limitations of label cautions and will bring significant added protection to our families and homes."

11

Helpers and Yelpers

IN HIS 1968 State of the Union message, the President of the United States stressed the importance of new legislation to protect the consumer. The 90th Congress, he indicated, might well become known as the consumer's Congress, and he pointed out that there should be effective laws to insure the safety of meat, fish and drugs for human consumption. These laws in some states are considered inadequate.

To enforce the Federal food and drug laws, the FDA in 1968 employed about 4,700 people in Washington and throughout the country, including administrators, inspectors, BDAC agents, scientists, consumer education specialists and clerical help. More are needed, particularly if and when the agency is required to perform added duties, and consideration will be given to the appointment of scientists in the following major specialties:

162

Bacteriology.
Chemistry (including Biochemistry)
Entomology.
* Food and Drug Inspection.
Medical Biology Technician.
Medical Technician.

Medicine.
Microanalysis.
Microbiology.
Pharmacology.
Physical Science Aid.
Veterinary Medicine

* A B.S. degree with thirty semester hours in any of the biological sciences, physical sciences or pharmacy satisfies the academic requirement for Food and Drug Inspection. Examinations are open to students in the junior and senior years of college.

All positions are filled from lists of names of people who have qualified in competitive civil-service examinations for particular fields. Information about examinations can be obtained from the U. S. Civil Service Commission, Washington, D. C. 20415, or from many post offices. Applicants may also wish to visit FDA district offices, which are located in:

Atlanta, Georgia.
Baltimore, Maryland.
Boston, Massachusetts.
Buffalo, New York.
Chicago, Illinois.
Cincinnati, Ohio.
Dallas, Texas.
Denver, Colorado.
Detroit, Michigan.

Kansas City, Missouri.
Los Angeles, California.
Minneapolis, Minnesota.
New Orleans, Louisiana.
New York, New York.
Philadelphia, Pennsylvania.
San Francisco, California.
Seattle, Washington.

Each summer the FDA appoints student assistants (temporary) and student trainees (permanent) under a program designed to attract college students to return as permanent employees upon completion of their academic studies. You can obtain more specific information about this program by writing to the Personnel Office, Food and Drug Administration, Washington, D. C. 20204.

Any scientist or specialist who accepts a position in a government regulatory agency such as the FDA will find that he or she is part of an organization that may be the target of various critics who disagree with certain policies. Some of the Federal food and drug regulations have met with strong opposition from pharmaceutical and medical groups. It isn't the purpose of this book to support one side or another, but a description of some of the differences is included here because it illustrates the point and is considered to be an important part of the FDA story.

For one thing, much publicity has been given to the matter of prescribing drugs by their generic (genus or general class) names in preference to trade or brand names. A clear explanation of the difference has been made by the Pharmaceutical Manufacturers Association (PMA), a nonprofit scientific, professional and trade organization dedicated to the encouragement of high standards of drug potency, quality and purity, and of research to develop new, better and safer pharmaceutical products. Its members are about 140 firms producing prescription drugs. As explained by the PMA:

> Most drug products have three names—the *chemical* name, the established or *generic* name, and the *trademark* or *brand* name. The first two names describe the same thing —that is, the chemical composition of the active therapeutic ingredient(s). The first is scientific and precise; the second is more convenient and concise. The relationship is analagous to that of the scientific term, *Homo sapiens,* and the more common and usable term, *man.* The third name—the trademark or brand name—on the other hand, refers to a particular manufacturer's formulation, and identifies the drug product with the originator or manufacturer. So the

completed analogy would go like this: *Homo sapiens,* man, John T. Jones.

As a specific example, the *chemical* name of one diuretic (a drug used to decrease excessive fluids in the body) is: 6-chloro-3, 4-dihydro-7-sulfamoyl-2H-1,2,4, benzothiadiazine-1, 1 dioxide.

Says the PMA:

Obviously a drug compound must also have a shorter, more usable name. Such a name is originated by research or medical authorities involved in the possible therapeutic application of the chemical. The name is then submitted to review committees of the American Medical Association and of two standard drug references, the *U. S. Pharmacopeia* and the *National Formulary.* These three groups function through a coordinating group called "The United States Adopted Names Council." If there is any conflict with existing names, or disagreement as to the meaning suggested by the proposed name, further negotiation takes place with the initial sponsor of the name. The Food and Drug Administration has veto power over final selection. If entirely satisfactory, the name is then transmitted to the World Health Organization, which works with the official pharmacopeial organizations of many nations.

What happens when the name is approved and ready for use? "It is thereafter known as the 'established' name, also referred to as the 'generic,' 'official,' or 'nonproprietary' name; the most popular of these terms being 'generic'."

In the case of the chemical tongue-twister mentioned in the foregoing, the established or generic name adopted was hydrochlorothiazide. This name, of course, does not tell if the product is uncrystallized, crystalline, coarse or fine, and does not describe its degree of purity beyond minimum legal standards. In proper use, the term "generic name" refers to the active chemical ingredient, not to the finished product. To be dispensed and used, the chemical ingredient must be combined with other inactive substances and made into a form such as a pill, an ampule or a suppository.

The next step, says the PMA, is selection of the brand name or trademark:

> Pharmaceutical companies generally adopt brand names or trademarks to identify their products. No official rules control this nomenclature. The objective is to coin a name which is useful, dignified, easily remembered, and individual or proprietary. One manufacturer of a product based on hydrochlorothiazide gave its finished product the brand name *HydroDIURIL*, suggesting partly the chemical name and partly its diuretic properties. Another manufacturer, for other reasons, chose to name its product containing hydrochlorothiazide ESIDREX; a third, ORETIC.

After a named drug is put into use in interstate commerce, the brand name is generally registered as a trademark with the U. S. Patent Office.

Many people who protest high drug prices have argued that if doctors prescribed drugs by generic names, patients could buy such drugs at prices much lower than the same drugs would cost when sold under brand names.

Opponents insisted that there were important differences in generic-name drugs of the same kind, and that physicians should be free to prescribe drugs by brand name if they believed that the trademark provided an added assurance of the specific ingredients they wanted their patients to have.

Helpers and Yelpers

Eugene N. Beesley, as chairman of the board of the Pharmaceutical Manufacturers Association, commented on this subject in a statement to a Senate Subcommittee on Antitrust and Monopoly headed by the late Senator Estes Kefauver in 1961.

MR. BEESLEY: Those who advocate generic prescribing overlook the fact that there can be important variations between drugs with the same generic therapeutic agent. They can have different inactive ingredients and special excipients [inert substances used to give drugs a certain form of pleasant taste], vehicles and bases. They can be buffered to promote tolerance or be made sugar-free for the diabetic. The therapeutic agent can be released at varying rates of speed. These variations often produce important differences in medical results. This consideration cannot be taken into account when generics are prescribed, because the generic name identifies only the active ingredient in a medicine and not the finished pharmaceutical product. Physicians can identify these important variations by the manufacturer's brand name or trademark. Because of these differences, it is most desirable that the physician know exactly what drug his patient has taken so that he can assess its value and chart his future treatment of the patient accordingly. . . .

It is also important to recognize that the brand name, on which the manufacturer stakes his reputation, serves as a powerful incentive for him to strive for a high degree of excellence.

With respect to the high prices of drugs Mr. Beesley said:

Some appear to assume that there is a magic in generic-name products which produces low prices. This is not so. Certain companies selling their products by generic name offer a limited number of drugs at prices below those of other companies. These lower prices are possible only because the companies offering them undertake none of the risk and expense involved in research, clinical testing, and informing the medical profession in the use of products they sell. Every one of these products has already been discovered, developed, and established—scientifically, medically, and commercially—at the expense of someone else. . . .

At this point, however, it is significant to note that in December, 1967, three major drug manufacturers were convicted for conspiring to rig drug prices over a ten-year period.

I talked with one doctor who had served in the armed forces a few years ago and who had then used generic-name drugs purchased under Federal government contracts. "I discovered," he said, "that some of these drugs were not as satisfactory and didn't perform in the same way as their brand-name equivalents."

Later I learned that since his experience, the Department of Defense has instituted a program under which only drugs of the highest quality are used in the treatment of our military and naval personnel. The Department of Defense has a Defense Military Materiel Board whose members are the Surgeons-General of the various services, and a staff of more than one hundred pharmacists, chemists, and other technically qualified experts, working at the Defense Personnel Support Center in Philadelphia, Pennsylvania.

A description of the board's procedures was furnished to the Senate Monopoly Subcommittee of the Select Committee on Business by Congressman Durward C. Hall in 1967. As Dr. Hall, once a practicing physician, pointed out, "The board's task is to decide what drugs are needed in the military and, further, to set up very detailed specifications for each

one of them. . . . The Department usually designates the drugs it requires by generic name, but does not buy 'generic products'. When they use the generic term, they refer to those products which meet the very rigid specifications they have set up."

The Department's precise specifications are proposed before any bids are invited and before the matter of price is considered. When bids are received, the Department may undertake a survey of the plants of possible suppliers, and its experts go over the plant to make sure the company is capable of producing a high-quality product.

"During the fiscal year 1966," Congressman Hall revealed, "160 such surveys were carried out. Rather shocking is the fact that 46 percent of the plants inspected were found to be unacceptable. Since January, 1962, when the inspection program began, more than 350 plants have been rejected; that figure, I emphasize, represents nearly half of the 780 plants visited."

In addition to the plant surveys, the Department of Defense requires potential contractors to submit samples of their drugs before a contract is awarded, and the samples are carefully analyzed by the Department's own medical laboratory.

Adds the Congressman, "This is all in addition to FDA clearance, which is a requisite before a product becomes marketable in the first place."

If a military doctor wants to obtain a brand-name drug that is not in the normal distribution channels, he may do so if he feels that his patient needs it.

Dr. Hall made another important point. "Trusting devotees of a wishful dream," he said, "will say that all drugs are alike; that tetracycline is tetracycline; that a pill is a pill; that

there is such a thing as 'generic equivalency'. The experience of the best minds in medicine is to the contrary. The medical literature is replete with testimony that shows that 'generic equivalency' is nonsense."

To back up this assertion he quoted a statement made by FDA Commissioner Goddard on this question: "I think it's going to require very careful study before anyone could assume that there is such a thing as generic equivalency on a broad scale in our drug field today. There will have to be better methods of determination of equivalency than we now have, and more attention to the entire problem. It's not a simple issue. We appreciate this." But Dr. Goddard also has said he believes there is equivalency among most drug products that meet established specifications.

Dr. Hall furnished the senators with specific examples showing that in a number of hospitals the use of generic-name drugs produced serious side effects that were not evident when brand-name drugs were used.

In praising the program of the Department of Defense to insure the purchase of high-quality drugs, he said, "Responsible drug companies have nothing to fear from such a program. Should they not be able to prove that their products work, I seriously question their right to supply drugs to anyone. Such firms have no business in this business. They should not be in any way associated with drugs, because *life* may depend on drugs. Such firms should make hula hoops and wastebaskets, not drugs. They deserve neither the business of sick patients nor the encouragement of physicians or Congressional committees. They most emphatically do not now get the recognition of most American doctors. . . . If reputation, resources and ability to produce are not of

importance in the drug field, they count for nothing any-where else."

Even with brand-name products, some advertisers fail to show all the side effects their drugs may produce, or may make claims that might mislead physicians who prescribe the drugs. Many arrows have been aimed at the FDA for cracking down on such misleading advertising.

As this book was being written, dark clouds were gathering for what threatened to engulf the FDA, the drug industry and the medical profession in a controversial storm of hurri-cane force. Here are the elements: From 1938 to 1962, FDA regulations required only that drugs must meet specified safety factors. In 1962, following the Kefauver drug hear-ings, Congress amended the Food, Drug and Cosmetic Act to provide, among other things, that drug manufacturers had to show not only that drugs were *safe* for human use, but also that they were *effective* for their intended purposes.

In 1966 Commissioner Goddard arranged for the National Research Council–National Academy of Sciences to under-take a careful study of about three thousand drugs appear-ing under about sixteen thousand trade names that were marketed between 1938 and 1962 (when the law was amended). Certain patent medicines were included, along with many "old family favorites that may be less than the best."

The study is being made by twenty-nine panels of two hundred medical and pharmaceutical specialists, whose re-ports were expected to be submitted to the FDA periodically throughout 1968 and into 1969.

Dr. Goddard has explained that the drugs would be

divided into four classes of effectiveness: (1) effective; (2) probably effective; (3) possibly effective; and (4) ineffective. "Those found to be ineffective will be ordered off the market immediately," he said. The "probables" and "possibles" will be further investigated. He estimated that perhaps 10 percent of the three thousand drugs under study would be found ineffective.

He also predicted that some results of the study might be attacked by some members of the health and pharmaceutical industries, and he expected that the FDA would get numerous complaints from physicians who may find that they can no longer prescribe certain drugs with which they have been treating their patients.

Dr. Goddard makes the important point that in the United States we have roughly 150 physicians for every 100,000 people. "They prescribe drugs and presumably keep track of results," he says, "but their patient load is heavy and their ability to see all aspects of any single drug's effectiveness is severely limited. We must therefore cast a very wide net in order to catch the full range of effectiveness of any one drug or group of drugs. No one physician, no one medical school or school of pharmacy, no single hospital system or insurance carrier can support this kind of monitoring program, although every one of these can contribute to it and needs to draw upon it."

In fairness he adds, "That, of course, is one aspect of the efficacy issue as it has been raised. The individual practicing physician has sometimes been singled out as the best possible judge of a drug's efficacy, whereas the judgments of the Food and Drug Administration, which collects and organizes drug data as part of its mission, are held in some suspicion.

I will not argue our infallibility; we don't have it, and that's that. But there is no other agency available to medical practice today that can draw upon the experiences of drug prescribers and users scattered throughout the United States and its territories."

While there are controversies between the FDA and many drug manufacturers, it must not be inferred that the latter are opposed to all FDA activities. When the FDA was given new duties as a result of amended laws, the President asked Congress for increased FDA funds to perform these duties. While the budget request was being considered by the Health Subcommittee of the Senate Appropriations Committee, the Pharmaceutical Manufacturers Association sent a letter to the subcommittee reading in part: "On occasion, when our association and its member firms perceive a valid difference with FDA in the interpretation of a statute or a regulation, we do not hesitate to speak out in behalf of our position. This should not indicate, however, that we disagree in any way with the basic importance of the agency's responsibilities to the scientific and industrial communities and to the public. We consider the President's request for financing . . . reasonable and realistic in view of the needs to administer and enforce existing and anticipated laws. We respectfully urge your subcommittee's approval of the proposed budget."

An outburst of criticism was directed against FDA Commissioner Goddard as a result of remarks he reportedly made at a press conference in New Jersey City on December 30, 1967. In discussing useful and useless drugs, the commissioner was quoted in newspaper stories as saying that "the

corner drugstore should be closed down." The National Association of Retail Druggists retorted that Dr. Goddard was
the one who should close down—resign, that is.

I invited the National Association of Retail Druggists to
comment on its attitude toward the FDA, for publication in
this book, but my invitation received no response.

An editorial in the St. Louis, Missouri, *Post-Dispatch* had
this to say about Dr. Goddard's remarks:

> We are sure Dr. Goddard yields to no man in his regard
> for that great American institution, the drug store, whether
> it is on the corner or in the middle of the block. As we got
> his remark, it was a flash of rhetoric intended to convey the
> idea that Americans, a notoriously drug-saturated people,
> would be better off if it were not quite so easy for them to
> buy so many drugs that are ineffective or unneeded.
>
> As a matter of fact, it would not be at all amiss for drug-
> gists individually and the National Association [of Retail
> Druggists] all together to associate themselves with this
> sensible idea and join in weaning our somewhat hypochon-
> driacal society from drug taking as a form of reflex action.
> It would do as much to elevate the professional prestige of
> the pharmacist as the blather at Dr. Goddard is doing to
> lower it.

At the American Pharmaceutical Association (APhA) in
Washington, D. C., I talked with Mr. George Griffenhagen,
director of the Division of Communications. The APhA
membership consists only of individual registered pharmacists
—no stores or firms are members.

Mr. Griffenhagen explained that pharmacists sometimes
level criticism at the FDA because they are understandably
confused by reports that attempt to describe complex circumstances in oversimplified fashion. As an example he men-

tioned the Drug Abuse Control Amendment (DACA) list, a compilation of depressants, stimulants and hallucinogens covered by FDA regulations.

"When the first DACA list was announced," he said, "three tranquilizers were included. A hearing was held incident to the proposed regulations. Meprobamate (known as Equanil and Miltown) was to be covered, but the manufacturer announced that he would seek a court action to exclude this drug. Legal steps may therefore result in action that will keep meprobamate off the DACA list. However, pharmacists are confused because the FDA has said that meprobamate is to be covered by the regulation, but that later it might not be. This represents only one kind of situation in which pharmacists criticise the FDA. Then, when they get a full explanation of the circumstances, most of them agree that the matter is complex and that much of the criticism is unwarranted."

Trying to keep its members fully and accurately informed on pertinent subjects is an important task of the APhA, and this was emphasized after the news stories appeared about "closing down the corner drugstore." Instead of jumping in to join the attacks on Dr. Goddard, the APhA arranged for the executive committee of its board of trustees to confer with him to get a clarification of his remarks. Dr. Goddard explained that he envisioned the pharmacist of the future as a "therapy advisor." His further comments, as published in *The APhA Newsletter* for the information of all members, were these:

The Therapy Advisor would be the person who would discuss with the patient the medicine he is going to take, its possible adverse effects, the specific contraindications regarding other drugs, foods, and so on. He would be the point of contact for any problems related to the therapy and would obviously report adverse reactions to a Central Clearing House. In addition, the Therapy Advisor would be the source of information on new drugs as they become available. In this way, I feel the professional expertise of the pharmacist could be best made use of in our society, which is becoming desperately short of skilled health personnel.

The APhA followed this quotation in the *Newsletter* by its own comment:

While the Association has not always agreed with the Commissioner, the Executive Committee of the Board of Trustees does not believe that the impromptu and sketchy discussion during the New York press conference should be used to discredit Dr. Goddard's ideas or him.

As an example of the cooperative spirit that exists between the APhA and the FDA, Mr. Griffenhagen pointed to a National Conference on Public Education in Drug Abuse sponsored jointly by the APhA and the FDA in January, 1968. The conference brought together more than 150 representatives from the professions, from government, educational, youth and service organizations to exchange information and ideas on how best to combat the growing menace of drug abuse through public education.

Mr. Griffenhagen said that the APhA was interested not only in what the FDA did in connection with drug regulations, but also in what it did *not* do—and should. For one thing, he pointed out, there are many nonprescription drugs whose labels fail to show quantities of the active ingredients used in the drugs. The APhA publishes and sells a *Hand-*

book of Non-Prescription Drugs which lists drugs along with ingredients and quantities where they are known—but many manufacturers have refused to supply this information. As the Introduction to the *Handbook* says:

> It seems incredible that all standard drug information sources either completely ignore or include only a very limited number of examples of formulas and evaluations on use, toxicity and contraindications of products for home medication. This despite the fact that surveys have indicated that *as many as twenty per cent of all adverse drug reactions originate from the use of over-the-counter products.* . . . [Italics supplied.]

A pharmacist is often the first professional person consulted by a man or woman with a cold, a stomachache, a headache or some other ache, pain or malady. Former Surgeon General Leroy E. Burney of the U. S. Public Health Service said of the pharmacist: "He has a distinct contribution to make in assuring that self-medication achieves its greatest good and least possible harm through his explanation, advice, and warning."

The APhA *Handbook* says:

> To achieve this potential, the American Pharmaceutical Association has proposed the legal reclassification of drugs in the United States into four categories. These are:
> 1. Drugs to be dispensed on prescription order and renewable at the prescriber's direction only.
> 2. Drugs to be initially dispensed on prescription order only, but renewable at the pharmacist's discretion.
> 3. Drugs to be dispensed personally by the pharmacist at the request of the patient.

4. Drugs to be directly available to the public without professional direction or control.

Without knowing the quantities of active ingredients in nonprescription drugs, a pharmacist is seriously handicapped in giving advice to customers who seek self-medication. The APhA hopes that FDA will take action that requires quantities to be shown on labels, but says that thus far the FDA has not done so.

Mr. Griffenhagen mentioned another area that needs strengthening. "How can a pharmacist decide whether any particular drug product is good or bad if he doesn't know who manufactured the dosage form as well as the therapeutic substance?" he asks. "There's no requirement for such detailed information to be included on a drug label, whether the drug is identified by generic name or by trademark name. A drug might be made by one firm and sold to a repacker who, in turn, might sell the product to a distributor who finally puts his name on the label."

The APhA believes the public and the prescribing and dispensing professions have a right and a need for complete information about a drug product. The FDA claims that special legislation is needed for any such requirements, but the APhA points out that the FDA has not lent full support to the introduction of such legislation.

To broaden the scope of this book, I asked the American Medical Association to comment on its attitude toward the work of the FDA with respect to drugs and doctors, but the AMA said only that it did "not care to express an opinion." A similar invitation to an association of frozen-food packers, with respect to FDA food regulations, also failed to get any response.

Finally, I did get some comment from FDA Commissioner Goddard about some of the subjects discussed in the foregoing pages. For one thing, I asked him whether he believed that trade-name drugs were more dependable than those using generic names.

"It's really irrelevant to the FDA whether a drug is sold under its generic name or a brand name," he said. "Our responsibility is to assure that *all* drugs on the market meet quality standards. We find deficiencies in drugs made by small companies and large, in drugs sold by generic name and by brand name. The question of therapeutic equivalency is always a complex one, however. Are two drug products meeting the same physical specifications, with the same active ingredients, equally effective when used in treating the patient? Generally, I believe they are. There may be exceptions, however. We're sponsoring a series of clinical studies now that I hope will provide a clear-cut answer."

Considering the wide scope of FDA's responsibilities, I asked whether the agency needed more people and equipment.

"I don't suppose there's any agency in government, or a private firm for that matter, that couldn't use more personnel and equipment to good advantage," Dr. Goddard answered. "But one of our primary needs is more than a budget problem, and that's the need for physicians in our Bureau of Medicine. It's always extremely difficult to recruit medical officers for government service. Since the middle of 1966 we've had some sixty-five Public Health Service physicians working in FDA. This enabled us to eliminate a backlog of 'new drug applications' which had built up since passage of the Drug Amendments of 1962. But these PHS officers will complete their two-year tours of duty in July of 1968, and finding replacements for them so we can effectively carry out our medical responsibilities will be a real challenge."

On occasion I had heard references to "the drug lobby." I asked Dr. Goddard what it was. "I suppose you're referring to the efforts of drug manufacturers and their associations to present their views to the Congress as persuasively as they can. Most industries engage in this kind of activity, and that's their right. Congressional committees normally hear many different points of view when considering legislation or conducting investigative hearings. Perhaps what's needed, however, is a more effective 'lobby' for the consumer, so that his views will also be presented as effectively as possible."

There has been considerable newspaper and magazine publicity concerning the sale and use of pills by people who want to lose weight. When I asked for Dr. Goddard's comment on obesity pills, he provided me with a copy of a statement on the subject which he made before the Senate Subcommittee on Antitrust and Monopoly.

"First," he said, "let me say that there are no drugs that can safely control the problem of obesity. There is no easy, painless way for an overweight person to eat what he or she wants and to melt off excess fat by taking one or a dozen drugs a day."

Dr. Goddard's statement to the committee centered on thyroid-digitalis combination drugs. "In our view," he said, "these combinations are both irrational and dangerous when dispensed for weight reduction."

I asked Dr. Goddard what the average citizen can do to

help the FDA. "He can best help the FDA—and himself— by being an alert consumer," the commissioner said. "Too often people don't read labels on nonprescription drugs, on food products or on household products that carry warnings and specific directions for use. This label information is important, not only to help consumers make shopping selections that best meet their needs, but also for the protection of health. Consumers shouldn't be timid about asking questions when they need information, or in making complaints when a product is misrepresented or proves to be unsafe. The FDA is receptive to consumer reactions—in fact, we need them to be effective in carrying out our responsibilities." *

In other words, the success of the FDA's efforts depends to an important extent upon the cooperation of the public— you and me and the folks next door. The unscrupulous food processor, the crafty advertiser, the health quack and their kind prosper primarily because their victims are careless or gullible. An informed public is the greatest obstacle to the success of any racket.

Of course, thousands of unfortunate people will go on being victimized and hurt. Perhaps they can find some degree of consolation in the fact that even our United States Government itself was a sucker for some modern medicine man. Early in 1968 it was revealed that Uncle Sam had paid $24,000 for 24,000 bottles of "physiological sodium chloride," a special saline solution for laboratory use. Imagine all the government faces that turned red when it was later discovered that the bottles contained ordinary seawater!

---

* *Dr. Goddard resigned as Commissioner of the FDA, effective June 30, 1968, after this book was written.*

SOURCES OF FURTHER INFORMATION

American Pharmaceutical Association
  2215 Constitution Ave., N. W.
  Washington, D. C. 20037

Committee on Interstate and Foreign Commerce
  House of Representatives
  Washington, D. C. 20515

Food and Drug Administration
  200 C Street, S. W.
  Washington, D. C. 20204

Pharmaceutical Manufacturers Association
  1155 15th Street, N. W.
  Washington, D. C. 20005

Special Committee on Aging
  United States Senate
  Washington, D. C. 20510

U. S. Public Health Service
  Bethesda, Maryland 20014

INDEX

Abunda Products, Inc., 143
Accidents, household, 148-161
Additives, food, 43-45
Adulteration, food and drug, 12
Aging, Senate Commtitee on, 71
Agriculture, U. S. Department of, 15, 19, 21, 28-29, 52, 71, 92
American Academy of Pediatrics, 70
American Medical Association, 70, 146, 165, 178
American Pharmaceutical Association, 174-178
Amphetamines, 97-114
Andre, John, 75
Andreadis, John T., 75, 77-79
Animal drugs and feeds, 93-94
APhA Newsletter, The, 175-176
Army General Depot, New York, 59
Arthritis and Rheumatism Foundation, 131
Arthritis remedies, 130-132

Aspirin, 89
Assize of Bread, 11

Baby food, contaminated, 37-38
Barbiturates, 97-114
Bartels, Judge John R., 79
"Bean cleaner," 39
Beesley, Eugene N., 167-168
Bellevue Hospital (New York), 123
Better Business Bureaus, 75
Biologic drugs, 92
Bologna, G. J. (Jack), 105, 108, 110, 119, 125-27
Botulism, 35-37
Brand names, drug, 164-170
British Medical Journal, 91
Burney, Dr. Leroy E., 177

Cal-Tex Company, 53-57
Cancer remedy, 134-138
Caveat emptor, 14
Center for Treatment and Education on Alcoholism, 113

185

Chicago meat-packing houses, 18-19
Child Protection Act of 1966, 156, 161
"Citizenship and the Strawberry Jam," 64
Civil Service Commission, U. S., 113, 163
Collier's Weekly, 17
Colors, cosmetic, 62-63
Colors, food, 45
Consumer Services Staff, FDA, 64-65
Contaminated food, 30-42
Cooper Hospital, 31
Cornell University Medical College, 123
Cosmetics, harmful, 61-64
Counterfeit drugs, 102-104
Crackerballs, explosive, 10, 157-158
Crampeze, 139
Creatine, 135-136

Defense, Department of, 168-169
Devices, quack medical, 139-147
Diet fads, 68-70
Dimethyltryptamine (DMT), 177
Dolls, flammable, 158
Doubleday, Page & Co., 18
Drug Abuse Control, Bureau of (BDAC), 101
Drug Abuse Control Amendments, 101, 121, 174
Drug dangers, 80-27
Drug inspections, FDA, 84-85
Drug labels, 84-86
Drug lobby, 180
Drug prices, 166-168
Drug Research Corp., 74-79

Drugs, counterfeit, 102-104
Drugs, generic names of, 164-170
Drugs, new, 86-90
Durovic, Dr. Stevan, 134-135, 137
Durovic, Marko, 134, 137

Eggs, spoiled frozen, 47
Elderly people, frauds affecting, 71-73
Electrometers, Hubbard, 141
"Elixirs of life," 13-14
"Enriched" foods, 52
Ergot, 116
Evening Post, New York, 18

Fair Packaging and Labeling Act, 48
FBI, 114
Federal Hazardous Substances Labeling Act, 148-150
Federal Register, 157
Federal Security Agency, 21
Federal Trade Commission, 75, 146
Finlator, John, 114
Fireworks, 159-160
Fish, counterfeit, 48
Flash point, 154
Flood, Rep. Daniel J., 22, 103-104
Flounder, poisoned, 31-35
Fogarty, Rep. John E., 22
Folic acid, 31
Food, contaminated, 30-42
Food, Drug and Cosmetic Act, 21, 43, 57, 62, 67, 75, 88, 101, 145, 171
Food, Drug and Insecticide Administration, 21
Food additives, 43-45
Food and Drug Act, 19-21, 62

Food colors, 45
Food-handling precautions, 41
Food labels, 47-53
Food standards, 51-52
Fort, Dr. Joel, 113
Founding Church of Scientology, 141

Gadgets, health, 139-147
Gas chromatograph, 29
Gehm, Susan K., 145
Generic names of drugs, 164-170
Georgia Power Co., 125
Ghadiali, Dinshah P. F., 144-145
"Giant quart," 49
Goddard, Dr. James L., 22, 86, 170-176, 179-180
Good Housekeeping, 17
Grades, food, 52
Grain Sanitation Program, FDA, 31
Griffenhagen, George, 174, 176, 178

Hair dyes, 62
Hall, Rep. Durward C., 168-170
Hallucinogens, 115-127
Handbook of Non-Prescription Drugs, 176-177
Hanover (Ind.) College, 14
Harvard University, 15, 78, 120
Hazardous Substances Act, 156, 161
Hazards, home, 148-161
Health, Education and Welfare, Department of, 11, 21, 157
Health quacks, 66-79
Heroin, 124
Herrick, Arthur D., 75, 77
History of Drugs, The, 12

Hofman, Dr. Albert, 118
Hospital Reporting System, FDA, 88
"How Safe Is Our Food?", 65
Howard, R. J., 40-41
Hubbard E-meters, 141

Indiana Medical College, 14
Insecticides, 28-30
Inspections, FDA drugs, 84-85
Internal Revenue Service, 114, 137
Ivy, Dr. Andrew C., 134-135, 137

Johns Hopkins University, 91
Johnson, President Lyndon B., 156
"Jumbo Pound," 49
Jungle, The, 18

Kastor, Hilton, Chesley, Clifford & Atherton, Inc., 75
Kefauver, Sen. Estes, 167
Kefauver-Harris Amendments, 89, 120, 129, 135
Kelsey, Dr. Frances O., 90-92
Kennedy, President John F., 92
Kevadon, 90, 92
"Kickapoo Indian Sagwa," 14
King John, 11
Kleinschmidt, Dale, 31-35
Krebiozen, 134-138
Krebiozen Research Foundation, 136

Label, Regimen Tablets, 74
"Label" defined, 48
Labeling, deceptive nutritional, 67-70
Labeling of hazardous substances, 149-161

Labels, cosmetic, 62-63
Labels, drug, 84-86
Labels, food, 47-53
Labor, Department of, 114
Ladies' Homes Journal, The, 17
Laws, food and drug, 14-21
Lead oxide, 38-40
Lewin, Louis, 118
Liefcort, 128-129
Livestock, drugs for, 93-94
Louria, Dr. Donald B., 123
LSD, 10, 115-127
Lysergic acid diethylamide (LSD), 115-127

Marijuana, 119, 124
Master Violet Ray, 144
Mayer, Dr. Jean, 78
Meat Inspection Act, 19
Medical Quackery, First National Congress on, 146
Medical quacks, 128-147
Medicines, early patent, 13
Mental Health, National Institute of, 121
Mescaline, 117
"Meth is Death," 124
Methamphetamine, 124-125
Micro-Dynameter, 141
Millpax, Inc., 132-133
Millrue tonic, 132-134
"Misbranding," 53
Monroe, Marilyn, 112

Names, drug, 164-170
Narcotics, Federal Bureau of, 92, 101, 114, 119
National Association of Retail Druggists, 174

National Cancer Institute, 135-136
National Formulary, 165
National Research Council-National Academy of Sciences, 171
Navy Food Laboratory, 60
New Drug Institute, 75, 77, 79
New Drugs, investigation of, 86-90
North Carolina Bureau of Investigation, 106, 109
"Nutritional quackery," 67

Old Borax, 16
Opportunities, job, in FDA, 162-163
Orange juice, adulterated, 53-57

"Package" defined, 48
Packaging, deceptive, 50
Pana (coin), 12
Paratyphoid bacillus, 24
Patent medicines, 13
Patent Office, U. S., 166
Paxton, Roy F., 132-134
Penicillin contamination, 81-83
Pep pills, 96-114
Pesticide residues, 28-30
Peyote, 117-118
Pharmaceutical Manufacturers Association, 164-168, 173
Pharmacopeia, U. S., 165
Phillips, Dr. William F. P., 134, 137
Phocomelia, 91-92
"Pillistics," 103
Plantation Extract Corp., 58-61
Poison Control Center, Philadelphia, 32
Poison Squad, 16
Poisoning, accidental, 149-156

Pomet, Pierre, 12
Post-Dispatch, St. Louis, 174
Post Office Department, 75-76, 146
Prescription drugs, unlawful sales of, 110-113
Preservatives, food, 13
"Protection of Human Life, The," 65
Psilocybin, 117
Public Health Service, U. S., 22, 27, 71, 92, 151, 177, 179
Publishers, pressure on, 17
Purdue University, 15

Quacks, health, 66-79, 139-147
Quacks, medical, 128-147

Racketeers, reject-egg, 47
Radiation monitoring, 27
Rado Pad, 140
Rankin, Winton B., 103-104
Regimen Tablets, 73-79
Roberts, Will H., 134
Roosevelt, President Theodore, 17-19

Safflower oil capsules, 66-67
St. Anthony's Fire, 116
St. John's-wort, 58-59, 61
Salmon, Dr. D. E., 24
Salmonella, 24-27, 160
Salmonellosis, 24-26
Sandoz Pharmaceuticals, 118, 120-121
Sauna baths, 143-144
Secret Service, U. S., 114
Seizures, FDA drug, reasons for, 94-96
Sherman, Rep. James S., 16

Short Weight Jim, 16
Sinclair, Upton, 18
Smith, Charlie, 109
Smith, Dr. Jean Paul, 118-119
Sodium nitrite poisoning, 32-35
Spectrochrome, 144-145
"Speed freaks," 125
Standards, food, 51-52
State Bureau of Investigation, North Carolina, 106, 109
Stilbestrol, 80-81
Stoll, Dr. Arthur, 118
Sun, New York, 16

Tasters, food, 11
Taussig, Dr. Helen B., 91
Thalidomide, 11, 90-92, 134
Tomatoes, moldy, 40-41
"Total diet," teen-age, 27
Toys, harmful, 157
Trade names, drug, 164-170
Tylosin, 81

"United States Adopted Names Council," 165
Unitrol, 69
"Uranium tunnels," 130

Vanilla extract, adulterated, 58-61
Virginia State Police, 109
Vitamins, 67-68, 70-73

Walsh, Jerry, 131
"Warner's Safe Cure For Diabetes," 14
Washington (D.C.) Police Department, 35
Weight control tablets, 73-79
Weight reducing fads, 66-69

Index

Wiley, Dr. Harvey Washington, 14-21, 42

Williams, Sen. Harris A., 71-72

Wonder Drug Co., 75

World Health Organization, 165

World's Work, The, 18

"Wrinkle removers," 63

X-33 waterproofing paint, 153-156

"Young Scientists Look At Food," 65

190

About the Author

Harry Edward Neal was born May 4, 1906, in Pittsfield, Massachusetts, but left there in 1925 to work for the Federal government as a stenographer. In 1957 he retired as Assistant Chief of the United States Secret Service, Treasury Department, to devote all of his time to free-lance writing. For his devotion to duty he was presented with the exceptional Civilian Service Medal, then the government's highest civilian award. Before his retirement he wrote magazine articles and short stories which appeared in *The Saturday Evening Post, Collier's, Esquire, Coronet, Pageant, Cosmopolitan, Family Circle* and some 25 other national magazines. Today he concentrates on the writing of both juvenile and adult books, though occasionally he produces magazine pieces as well. Harry Neal has conducted workshops in fiction and nonfiction at numerous writers' conferences, including those at Georgetown University, Washington, D. C.; Iona College, New Rochelle, N. Y.; LaSalle College, Philadelphia, Pa.; McKendree College, Lebanon, Ill.; and the Christian Writers' and Editors' Conferences at St. Davids, Pa. and Green Lake, Wisconsin. He is a member of The Authors League of America, and of the Children's Book Guild of Washington. His wife, Berniece Roer Neal, is also a professional writer, writing teacher and lecturer. The Neals live in Culpeper, Virginia, about 70 miles south of Washington, D. C.